*There is a Woman
I Want to Be, Lord . . .*

She never doubts your existence or strays from
your ways. She never fails people or herself,
or you.

She is an ideal wife. A perfect mother. A neighbor and friend everyone loves and respects. Yet
she is all this without sacrificing her own dreams.
I keep thinking this woman will turn up some
day, God. Wearing my clothes. Wearing my face.
But somehow she eludes me. I catch only
glimpses of her. I see just enough of her now
and then so that I don't despair entirely.

Lord, dear patient Lord—thank you for showing
me at least these fragments of the woman I
want to be!

HOLD ME UP
A LITTLE LONGER, LORD

*A new book of joy by America's best-loved
inspirational writer. With illustrations by
her daughter, Patricia Mighell.*

Bantam Books by Marjorie Holmes
Ask your bookseller for the books you have missed

HOLD ME UP A LITTLE LONGER, LORD
I'VE GOT TO TALK TO SOMEBODY, GOD
LORD, LET ME LOVE
NOBODY ELSE WILL LISTEN
TO HELP YOU THROUGH THE HURTING
TWO FROM GALILEE
WHO AM I, GOD?

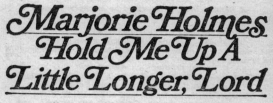

Marjorie Holmes
Hold Me Up A
Little Longer, Lord

Illustrated by Patricia Mighell

BANTAM BOOKS
TORONTO · NEW YORK · LONDON · SYDNEY · AUCKLAND

*This low-priced Bantam Book
has been completely reset in a type face
designed for easy reading, and was printed
from new plates. It contains the complete
text of the original hard-cover edition.*
NOT ONE WORD HAS BEEN OMITTED.

HOLD ME UP A LITTLE LONGER, LORD

*A Bantam Book / published by arrangement with
Doubleday & Co., Inc.*

PRINTING HISTORY
Doubleday edition published March 1977

2nd printing . . . . . July 1977	4th printing . . February 1978
3rd printing . . November 1977	5th printing . . . . . . June 1978
6th printing . . . August 1978	

*A selection of the Doubleday Book Club, the Christian
Herald Bookshelf, and the Word Book Club.*

Portions of this book appeared in GUIDEPOST, FAITH &
INSPIRATION, BOOK SHORTS, CHRIST FOR THE NATIONS, *and*
WOMAN'S DAY.

"An American Woman's Prayer," first appeared in
LADIES HOME JOURNAL as *"An American Woman's
Bicentennial Prayer."*

*Bantam edition / April 1979
2nd printing . . . . . . May 1979
3rd printing . . . February 1980
4th printing . . . . October 1980
5th printing . . . . January 1982*

ISBN 0-553-22545-6

Published simultaneously in the United States and Canada

PRINTED IN THE UNITED STATES OF AMERICA

14 13 12 11 10 9 8

For my sister Gwen

To: Mom

From: Your daughter, Lynn
    A little pleasure reading
to help you through many
more birthdays to come.
        June of '88

Acknowledgments

This book is in response to the many requests that have been received from readers of the column, "A Woman's Conversations with God" as it appeared in *Woman's Day*. The author wishes to thank the publishers of *Woman's Day* for permission to reprint the majority of these prayers in book form. Special thanks are also due Rebecca Greer for her patience, insight and skill in editing these prayer columns.

Contents

Hold Me Up A Little Longer, Lord

The Woman I Want to Be

Listen, Lord . . .

There is a wife I want to be.

She is beautiful, Lord (never dishevelled, never in curlers), always poised and gay and exquisitely dressed. The pride of her husband, whether at a club dance or conducting the P.T.A.

And oh, she is so tactful, so considerate. She doesn't call him needlessly at the office, never bothers him with things that go wrong at home or imposes on him the burden of errands and grocery lists. And when he comes in she is always ready to listen and laugh and sympathize, no matter how she feels or how turbulent has been her day.

She never gets her feelings hurt, Lord, or picks a fight or holds a grudge. Never is jealous, never pines for things they can't afford . . .

I think of her wistfully, Lord, for her husband worships her. She deserves it. She's the wife I long to be.

There is a mother I want to be . . .

Patient and cheerful, firm in discipline, just in decisions, rich in self-control. She never yells at her children—or the neighbor's kids. Never acknowledges, even in her secret heart, that she is sometimes dismayed and disappointed at what she has produced.

Her home is a haven for young of all ages. The

cookie jar is always full, the supply of cold drinks and understanding inexhaustible. The little ones adore her, the older ones confide in her, for her wisdom is infallible, her guidance as gold.

She's the kind poets write songs about, great men pay tribute to.

I wish I could find her, Lord. She's the mother I long to be.

There is a career woman I want to be . . .

She is smart and successful without neglecting her family. She never takes her problems to the office or brings them home with her. She is efficient, she is charming. She achieves her ambitions without losing her friends or her femininity. She travels, she gets her picture in the paper, yet it never turns her head.

What a vision of loveliness she is—this career woman I yearn to be.

Lord, there is a neighbor, a friend I want to be . . .

She is generous, hospitable, kind. Never too busy to help people. Never too filled with herself to listen, really listen when somebody else needs to spill out her heart.

This woman never gossips and she doesn't compete. She couldn't care less who has the biggest house, the showiest flowers or drives the classiest car. To join the best clubs, have the smartest children or most successful husband—such things don't bother her.

I see her so clearly, Lord, if not in my mirror at least in my mind. She's the neighbor and friend I want to be.

* * *

There is a woman I want to be, Lord . . .

She never doubts your existence or strays from your ways. She never fails people or herself, or you.

She is an ideal wife. A perfect mother. A neighbor and friend everyone loves and respects. Yet she is all this without sacrificing her own dreams.

I keep thinking this woman will turn up some day, God. Wearing my clothes. Wearing my face. But somehow she eludes me. I catch only glimpses of her. I see just enough of her now and then so that I don't despair entirely.

Lord, dear patient Lord—thank you for showing me at least these fragments of the woman I want to be!

"Remember the Lilies"

I've been cross, Lord, and upset.

All these shoes to be whitened, these buttons to be sewed on . . . And the shopping. A son has outgrown his jacket, a daughter wants a new dress. And my husband's relatives are coming for Easter, and the house is a mess.

With so much to be done I almost begrudged the time for Good Friday services at the church.

But just as we were leaving for them our son reminded: "Don't forget the lilies." And I groaned, because I *had* forgotten the lilies we always send to his grandmothers.

Now we stand in the flower shop, my child and I. Regarding the lilies—the fragrant white satin lilies of whom you said: "They toil not, neither do they spin, yet Solomon in all his glory was never so arrayed."

Forgive me if I smile, even as I drink in their heady perfume. You know, Lord, I'm no placid lily. And what would happen to my family if I *didn't* toil and spin?

Yet these lilies . . . these lovely, tranquil lilies, who epitomize such trust. *Need you go at everything so hard?* they seem to ask. *As the father has created and cared for them, so he has created and will care for you and all those dear to you.*

* * *

4

Lord, thank you for this lesson of the lilies.

Help me to remember it as I go back to the shoes to be whitened . . . the house to be cleaned . . . the buttons to be sewed on . . .

Help me to remember the lilies, not only at Easter but every day.

A Song of Praise for Spring

This is just a little song of praise for spring, Lord, and the wonders it works in me. The way it makes me want to rearrange things, clean and decorate things—the house, the garden, myself!

It's as if your sunshine, spilling across the waking earth, spills through a woman's spirits too. Why else should I feel this mad urge to paint the bathroom (forsythia yellow), tidy up closets and cupboards, add more purple cushions of creeping phlox to the driveway?

There's a touch of April, Lord, in the lift all this bestows. To see shelves lined with gay new paper, canned goods in neat array, shoes submissive on their racks, garments weeded as neatly as the first daffodils.

I'm even inspired to "houseclean" in the manner of our mothers. Literally strip a room down to its bare branches and scrub it until it squeaks and gives off a tang as exhilarating as rain on little new leaves. Then haul (or browbeat men into hauling) furniture back—but all in new places so as to be surprised each time we sail in . . .

Or to get clothes in shape. Fix zippers, alter skirts, add or subtract belt, buckle or bow. Or to make the sewing machine sing into the night; or come home from shopping with a sense of beauty and bargains that make me feel in style with the shining new wardrobe of the world.

Best of all, Lord, spring inspires me to do some neglected housecleaning and refurbishing of my spirit.

Out with self-pity, old grudges, regrets. In with self-esteem . . . To refresh my own interior with a new supply of forgiveness and understanding, of goals and delights and dreams. To scatter these like seeds in the soil of myself and literally feel them grow.

Thank you, Lord, for all these sources of sunshine for a woman—all these ways to feel and celebrate spring.

Give Me a Generous Spirit

Give me generosity of spirit, God. True generosity of spirit so that I can be truly glad, and show it, when other people succeed.

It's not hard to share a recipe or a baby sitter. Not a bit hard to lend a neighbor a tablecloth or an egg. It's even kind of thrilling to come to somebody's rescue with your best bag or prized (if unpaid for) mink.

And for most of us sympathy comes easy. To lend an ear to a friend's troubles, be a tower of strength in times of illness or disaster . . . There's a heady drama about being needed; the heart feels proud of itself, it receives more than it gives.

But oh, Lord, how much harder it is to share an hour of joy, of triumph. To be genuinely proud of somebody else. To be generous with praise . . . When another woman's child has made the Honor Society or the football team, or starred in the school play. When her husband has won a big promotion. Or when she herself has done something important, something exciting. When the flags of her life are flying!

That's the true test of friendship, Lord. Not when we feel luckier and stronger, when we can reach *down* to help somebody. But when we feel less lucky, our importance threatened; when we've got to reach *up* to give.

Guard me against jealousy, God. Free me from envy. Flood my heart with genuine joy, and help me to show it, when my friends succeed.

Mother and Child

Forgive me, Lord, but I think that each woman who has ever carried a child carries her cross.

Her greatest treasure, yes, but also her heaviest burden.

Her concern for it, the weight of her love for it. Her worry when it's ill, her suffering when it is hurt. The agony when it turns away from her—or you—and seems sometimes to be so lost.

I think of Mary carrying her blessed burden. In exaltation, as even the humblest woman is exalted by carrying life; and even more because she knew that she was carrying the child of God . . . But also carrying the ultimate pain of him. His rejection, his final inevitable hour upon the cross.

For she was surely to be nailed with him there. To bleed with him, to die with him. And when he rose again, to rise with him! To have her faith restored, to know the greatest joy of her life when she found the stone rolled away.

That, surely is one of the greatest messages of Easter for mothers. That as we are crucified with our children in all their pain and seeming failure, so we too are uplifted when they at last walk free.

Her son triumphed as with faith, my child will triumph. Her burden was not carried in vain as with faith, mine will not be.

"Early in the Morning"

"And early in the morning on the first day of the week . . ."

I think of those words, Lord, as I lie here longing only to go back to sleep. For it is very early in the morning on the first day for me too. And I dread the whole business of getting people up and ready for the sunrise services.

Instead, help me to realize how lucky I am to have a family that is well and able to go. Help me to throw off the tempting coziness of these blankets and spring out of bed. To go down the hall calling people, not with impatience in my voice, but on a note of celebration:

"Happy Easter!"

For the minute I say those words a miracle occurs. My sluggish spirit is suddenly revived. Happiness floods me. In a small but very human way I taste the incredible joy that Mary and the other women must have felt at the tomb when the angel told them: "He is risen."

To rise—what a wonderful thing!

For it means that life triumphs over death and night and sleep. The sun rises in the sky, and the flowers and grasses rise up in its wake.

And we rise too. Flesh weak, protesting, yet we rise to the marvelous challenge of each new day.

And as that day progresses we rise again and again above our problems, above our pain. With you we have the strength to overcome all things.

Thank you for this joyful awareness so early in the morning on the first day of the week.

A Little Privacy

Please help me to achieve a little privacy, Lord.

I'm tired of being squashed in with other people, eating and sleeping and sharing everything with other people. Dear as they are to me, they don't recognize my need for a little space between us.

It is as if they are just all over me all the time, if not with themselves with their possessions. Even when they're out of the house their papers and books and toys and gear clutter every room. Even my bedroom, even my desk and the place where I sew.

And they not only drop things behind them, they raid *my* books and papers and possessions. Make off with my lipstick, my sweaters, my scissors, my portable typewriter, the magazine I wanted to read. I don't feel I really own a thing in this house except maybe the iron and ironing board (they don't bother those!). (Well, yes, my toothbrush maybe—but I'm not always sure about that.)

Lord, I realize this is probably all my fault. I haven't trained them properly and I feel guilty about it. And the guiltier I feel, the less able I am to contend.

But somehow I've got to achieve a little privacy. For my sanity and my own soul's peace. An escape hatch, some small retreat; a door I can lock, a couch I can claim, a desk nobody can ransack for paper for a book report—maybe even a phone of my own.

Please fire me with the determination and the ingenuity to achieve some privacy, Lord. And the will and the words to make my family understand. Please let them co-operate.

And now, having gotten this off my chest, let me also remember something: If I just live long enough I'll have privacy—whether I want it or not!

There are plenty of women who'd trade places with me in a minute. Women who've lost their husbands, whose children are gone. Privacy, complete privacy comes all too soon.

Thank you for that reminder, even as I struggle for a little privacy now.

Bathtime

No matter how busy I am, Lord, let me be thankful and find joy in bathing my baby—he's growing so fast. No longer tiny and helpless, almost lost in a long white nightie, but now full to my arms, with a rollicking will of his own.

Thank you for the sight of his back straight and sturdy in the tub, and the perfect peach globe of his head. (Please keep him always straight and strong.) For the sheer bright abandon of his antics—his mad splashing, his impassioned clutch of floating ship and ball. For the foolishness of a chewed washcloth dribbling daily down his chin, and the flirtatious peeking of his eyes over the tub's rim.

My son, Lord, my plump brazen elf of a son to be soaped and rinsed as he scolds and sings and chatters in his own expressive jargon. My son to be gathered warm and wet into a big towel, to be patted and powdered and oiled.

I lift him up in a joyous little gesture of offering, and he dances on tiptoe with nimble nakedness.

Thank you for this son to be wrestled into a diaper. For he keeps flopping over, scrambling to his knees—it is like trying to put pants on the wind! Yet you made mothers strong-fingered and determined. We must win the kicking contest against shoes and stockings, we must subdue our offspring into clothes.

And our reward is to carry a son at last, sweet and

fresh, clasping our neck, riding royally down to his dinner like a king.

Thank you for this child and this happy daily struggle that is half duty, half delight. And whenever it seems a chore, help me to remember how awfully fast little boys get too big to be bathed . . . or maneuvered into *any*thing.

The Other Cheek

"Turn the other cheek," the Bible says. "Pray for your enemies, return good for evil."

That's okay for saints, I used to think, but not for me. For a faulty, garden-variety struggler like me—well, it would be mission impossible. But I've tried it, Lord, and it works! On sheer impulse (or maybe some higher prompting) I've tried it—and something wonderful happens.

I never liked this woman, and I was positive she didn't like me. She said something unkind about me once—or so I was told. She had a big luncheon and didn't include me.

But yesterday I read that she's received an honor from her college for work she's done with underprivileged children. And suddenly, to my own amazement, I found myself writing her a note of congratulations.

My motive really wasn't very nice, Lord—I began almost grimly, taking pride in my own will power, in how "big" I could be. Then a strange and lovely change began to take place in me. I felt better about her even as I wrote, my pride in myself subtly changed to an honest pride in *her*. I was really glad for her, God, my own words that said so began to be true.

And today she called to thank me, and there was suddenly joy between us. A kind of shining affection! She asked me to have lunch with her.

She's really quite shy, I discovered—which must be why she seems aloof. (I wonder if she really said what the talebearer told me, or meant it in the way I took it if she did?) Anyway, my "enemy" is now my friend, Lord. And my only regret is that I waited so long to obey your commandment.

From now on I'm going to be quicker about turning the other cheek.

The New Outfit

Oh, Lord, dear Lord, I've spent too much on this new outfit. I'm beginning to worry even as I carry it excitedly down the street.

It's so lovely—the most becoming thing I've found in years. I felt I simply had to have it, and in one mad moment I bought it. But now the price tag is like a weight dragging at my steps. Guilt and anxiety are beginning to dim the first high delight I felt.

I see very nice looking things much more reasonable, it seems, in the windows I pass. I wince to recall what I paid, I deplore my rash impulse. I think of the bills, the budget, the things the children need.

What kind of mother am I to blow all that money on myself?

Lord, I am hesitating. Perhaps I should turn around right here before I lose my nerve and take it back! . . . Help me to do the right thing now, this minute, while the traffic light still says STOP . . . But no, it's turned to green, I'm somehow being propelled across the street, carrying my lovely box.

And my heart is suddenly lighter as a sweet conviction dawns: Anything cheaper that I didn't really *care* about would be a disappointment, not only to me but to the rest of them. They *want* me to feel and look the way I feel and look in this new outfit!

Thank you, Lord, for making me realize that now and then a woman simply has to be extravagant.

Help Me to Unclutter My Life

Help me to unclutter my life, Lord.

Rescue me from this eternal confusion of belongings (mine and other people's) that just won't stay orderly. This suffocation of phone calls, clubs and committees. ("No man can serve two masters," you said. A woman is lucky if she *has* only two!) This choke of bills and papers and magazines and junk mail. I buy too many things, subscribe to too many things, belong to too many things. The result is such confusion I can't really enjoy or do justice to anything!

Deliver me from some of this, Lord. Help me to stop bewailing this clutter and work out some plan for cutting down.

Give me the will power to stop buying things we don't really need and that only become a chore to take care of. Give me more sales resistance when it comes to antique stores and white-elephant sales and supermarkets. And give, oh give me the will power to get rid of a lot of things we already have. To unclutter my cupboards and closets and attic of things hung onto too long.

And oh, Lord, help me to unclutter my life of too many activities. Give me the self-discipline to stop joining things. And to weed out the organizations that don't really matter to me. (They'll be better off

without me.) And the strength to say "No!" more often when the telephone rings.

Lord, show me a way of uncluttering my life even of too many people without being unkind. A way to love and help people without letting them gobble me alive.

There are so many dear, wonderful people I long to see, need to be with for my own soul's growth. Yet we are lost to each other because of this profligate squandering of energy and time. Give me the determination to reclaim these truly life-strengthening friends, at whatever cost to other idle, meaningless relationships.

And while I'm at it, Lord, help me to unclutter my mind. Of regrets and resentments and anxieties, of idiotic dialogues and foolish broodings. Sweep it clean and free. Make it calm and quiet. Make it orderly.

Put me in control of it as well as my house . . . and my calendar . . . and my harried spirit. Thank you. With your help I know I can triumph, I can unclutter my life.

Give Me the Strength to Discipline

God, give me the strength to discipline my children.

Give me the love and the courage to lay down rules and see that they abide by them. Give me the ability to say "No!" when all my being longs to yield just because they want me to so much, or because I'd spare myself a lot of misery by saying "Yes."

Lord, help me to remember that children need the barriers of discipline to protect them from a world they're not yet ready for. And however loud they howl about "maturity" and "all the other kids" and "you don't trust me" and "you want to keep me a baby," in their secret hearts they're often thankful that the barriers are there. Even proud of having parents who care enough about them to say "No, you can't" and mean it. Help me to remember that this sort of caring gives them a sense of value that no amount of weak-kneed yielding to their every impassioned plea can match.

But oh, Lord, give me judgment in discipline so that I don't become a tyrant. Never let me discipline out of a sense of power and authority rather than a genuine concern for the welfare and happiness of my children.

Give me understanding too, and a sense of humor and fair play. Make me strong in discipline, Lord, but make me wise as well.

Chauffeur's Lament

This driving, Lord, all this driving.

Yes, I'm thankful to have a big active family, and thankful to still have a car and enough money (just barely) to pay for the liquid gold it guzzles. But sometimes I think if I have to set foot in that car another time *I'll* have a blowout, like one of the tires.

It's become my prison, Lord. A big dented, scratched, leather upholstered prison on wheels. And my sentence starts right after breakfast (or before) driving my husband to catch a plane or train or bus, driving kids to school. Even when it isn't my turn in the car pool there are a dozen different directions I've got to go to deposit people, pick up people, deliver things to people. And the minute school's out the directions double: To Little League and football practice, to Bluebirds and Y and horseback riding, to music and art and dancing lessons.

It doesn't even let up after dinner, the meetings only seem to multiply. And now that our son's old enough to date but not to drive, I've got to chauffeur him and his *girl*.

There's got to be a better method, God. Help me (or the government that keeps exhorting us to save fuel) to find it: More bicycles in the family? Cutting down, wherever possible on the activities and lessons?

(What good are advantages for children if they lack the advantage of a cheerful, fairly well-balanced mother?)

But until we find that method, please tank up my spirits for this job, and somehow bless this driving. Refuel my energies, pump up my sagging tires. Help me to remember the day will come when I'll be able to stay home more, have more time for myself. (And then I'll be worrying about *their* driving.)

Meanwhile, you know how grateful I really am, not only for my family but this car and my ability to drive it. So please forgive and make allowances for my chauffeur's lament.

Shopping with a Daughter

Lord, please give me strength for this shopping trip with my daughter.

Bless us both and let your love shine through us as we set off on what should be so pleasant, but is generally such an ordeal.

First, fortify me with thanksgiving. I realize I am lucky to have a lovely, healthy daughter who really enjoys clothes. And lucky to have enough money (if we don't go overboard) to provide the things she needs.

But I'm going to need some extra fortifying, Lord, with the following:

Please give me patience as we trudge from store to store, parade in and out of fitting rooms. (Ease my aching feet, soothe my frazzled nerves, keep sweet before me the picture of that hour when she finally finds *something* that meets with her approval.)

Give me will power. Don't let me show enthusiasm (if I like anything she's sure to shudder). Help me refrain from even making suggestions. No, however difficult, help me stand quietly by and let her choose.

Above all, don't let me talk her into things. And if I have to talk her *out* of things, please give me tact, let me be kind but firm. And let her accept my reasons without being too disappointed or resentful.

* * *

Give me good sense about price tags, God. Don't let me spoil her. But don't let me spoil our relationship either by being a pinchpenny mother.

Remind us both to smile at each other. To discuss instead of argue. To laugh when we're practically on the verge of blows. And to take time out for lunch or a cup of coffee. (It's when we both get tired that nerves and tempers flare.)

Thank you for giving us both strength for this shopping trip. For the joy and anticipation I suddenly feel. I'm smiling at her already, and she's smiling back! We do love each other enough to overcome our problems and appreciate our good fortune. We're setting off today to discover new delights.

Thank you that I can go shopping with my daughter!

The Party

This may seem a trivial thing to pray about—but please, Lord, go with me to this party.

Help me to stop being so nervous about meeting new people, or even being with people we don't see very often. Rid me of this silly, self-centered feeling that somehow I'm on trial.

Yes, I want to be a credit to my husband, our hostess—and to myself. But help me to stop worrying about my hair or what I'm wearing or what I'll say. Please, for heaven's sake, let me get it through my thick skull that nobody else *cares* in the slightest how my hair looks or how I'm dressed. Because most of them are simply too preoccupied with themselves. But that if I really want to be poised and confident and have a good time, I'll forget myself and just *be* myself. Above all, I'll take an interest in other people.

With your help I'm going to park my self-consciousness along with my wrap and start enjoying others—instead of just hoping and praying they'll enjoy *me*. I'm going to go up and speak to people instead of waiting for them to come to me. And if there is anyone else there as apprehensive, self-conscious and nervous as I am (until I turn to you) please lead me to them and let me make things easier and happier for them.

Give me courage, Lord. Give me a genuinely loving attitude so that the hours my husband and I spend with these people will be joyful, giving and good.

Good things begin to happen when we think of other people. . . . Good things are happening already. Thank you for going with me to this party.

The Priceless Company

This joy of women, Lord. This priceless company of women working together. Especially when the work that binds us is for people who really need what we can give. The sick, the old, the lonely. People whose problems are so much greater than our own. How wonderful, that in joining forces to help them we gain so much ourselves.

And the greatest of these is friends.

Sometimes, looking around me in a busy babbling room or hall or kitchen, a grateful tenderness fills me. Almost a sense of awe. These faces, all these faces—pretty and plain, young and old—yet every one of them alight with something lovely. Something warm. And every one of them dear to me, someone I can laugh with, talk with, share with as we work. And some of them special—grown such close friends over the years it would be hard to imagine life without them.

Thank you for the priceless company of all these kind, generous women, Lord. They are like a big dependable family. And I know that in my own time of trouble or crisis they would fly to my aid as well. They would support me, sustain me. I would never be alone.

How wonderful is this knowledge. Thank you that in reaching out to give a little help to others we are so rewarded. That we are given this priceless company.

The Stoning

Lord, I detest myself right now.

For I've just come from a luncheon where four of us spent most of our time criticizing a mutual friend. Her faults, her eccentricities, how extravagant and undependable she is. How she spoils her children, how vain and eager she always is to be attractive to men.

And though a lot of these things are true (Lord, they really are) I found myself wondering even as I joined in: Who are we to judge? Isn't every one of us guilty of at least some of the very same things? Was that why we attacked her with such relish? (Dear Lord, I'm so ashamed.) Because it made us feel a little bit better ourselves to brandish the defects of somebody so much "worse."

Well, I don't feel better about myself now. I keep thinking of what Jesus said to the men about to stone the adulterous woman: "Which of you is without sin?" Yet there we sat, self-righteous, stoning our sister with words.

How, Lord, can I make amends?

I long to call her up and beg her forgiveness, but that would be a terrible mistake. She would be so hurt, so much damage would be done. No, all I can do is to ask *your* forgiveness. And pray for her.

Help her, strengthen her, bless her. Don't let her ever know what we said about her, please.

And oh, Lord, put more compassion in my heart, guard my tongue. Don't let me ever again join in stoning a sister—or anyone—with words.

Good Roots

Help me to give my children good roots, God.

As I work with my plants I can see that the sturdiest, and those which bear most freely, are those whose roots go deep, gripping rich soil; they have a base from which they can grow tall and beautiful and sound.

Let this household furnish that kind of soil for my family, God. Enriched with good music, good books, good talk, good taste. But above all, goodness of spirit. Goodness of action.

So that those who come here feel welcome, and those who leave here feel warm. And those who live here know, in every fiber of their beings, that they belong to people who, for all our faults, are good people. People of decency and honor, who would not willingly hurt or cheat any living thing.

Let my children grow freely, God, in whatever direction their nature directs. But give them root strength, too. So that they will never deviate too far from their own beginnings.

Help me to give my children good roots.

"If Only"

Please rescue me, God, from the "if onlys."

If only my husband was home more, helped more, would try to be more understanding . . . If only the children would mind, cooperate, pick up after themselves, study harder, do better in school . . . If only my neighbors were more congenial . . . If only my friends were more considerate . . .

Then—ah *then* I'd be a happier person, able to be more efficient, productive, make my life really count.

Please help me to stop this blaming of outside circumstances, Lord, and start taking myself in hand.

And this includes bidding good-bye to the "if onlys" that keep beckoning me to look back:

If only I'd gone on to graduate school instead of getting married . . . If only I hadn't had my first baby so soon . . . If only I had encouraged my husband to go into business for himself . . . or *hadn't* discouraged him from buying that land (it's worth a fortune now) . . . If only . . . if only . . .

Lord, I know there's nothing more futile than these "if onlys." None of life's choices are guaranteed. The "mistake" of the past may have been a godsend in disguise. And we will never know, so how can we ever judge?

* * *

Only one thing is sure—that what we did or didn't do then, or what other people do or don't do now, has very little bearing on me. My happiness today.

So help me to shape up, Lord. To face my problems without the crutch of "if onlys" I've been leaning on.

Paper Boy

Oh, Lord, his alarm's gone off, I can hear it ringing
. . . ringing . . . as I lie here so snugly in bed. Please
let him hear it and get up without having to be called.
(Maybe if I just slipped in, without waking his
father . . .)

There now, thank you, he's stirring, it's stopped,
he's dressing. (Please let him put on a warm shirt and
his boots instead of sneakers, it's so cold, it's snow-
ing.)

Now his door is opening, I can hear him clumping
downstairs (thank you, Lord, that he's wearing his
boots). Please help him to find his heavy gloves
(they're right there on the hall table) and please,
please make him wear something on his head for a
change, that wind is fierce. (Maybe I should get up
and help him find it. Or try and persuade him . . .
And fix him some breakfast, only he'd probably have
a fit.)

Now he's getting his bike from the driveway. (I
can't help it, Lord, I just had to come to the window
to watch—and sure enough his head is bare, and the
bike's all covered with snow, he's got to brush it off
. . . Why, *why* won't he put it in the garage like he's
been told?)

Lord, help him, please help him as he lugs the
heavy bundle from the corner where it's been
tossed. And the wind's blowing so hard, help him as

he stuffs the papers into his bag and struggles the whole thing onto his shoulder. (Maybe I should throw on a coat and run down to give him a hand . . . Maybe I should even go with him.)

Should I, Lord? Tell me, help me . . . only it's too late anyway now. There he goes wobbling off down the snowy street. I might as well crawl back into my own warm bed . . . But, oh Lord, keep him safe. Don't let him get too cold or make too many mistakes this morning, and please get him back in time for a good hot breakfast before Sunday School.

And now, Lord, forgive me all this worrying. Let me go back to sleep knowing you will protect him, you are with him, you will put your loving arms around him.

Thank you that he wanted this job and for the lessons he's learning. Thank you, Lord, for my son and his paper route.

It's All Too Much

Oh, Lord, sometimes I feel it's all too much. My husband. The children. My job. This house.

The house is always ahead of me, I can't catch up. No matter how hard I work there is confusion and disorder wherever I look. "I need help!" I cry, but no help comes. Or it is brief, unsatisfactory, sometimes worse than before.

No, no, it's all up to me, and when I fail I despair of myself.

And the children. I am so often cross and unreasonable with them. But sometimes they drive me to distraction. Why do they misbehave? Why do they fight? Why don't they do better at school? We try to be good parents, and *this* is what we get, I think.

And my husband is always so busy. He doesn't understand me, I don't understand him. We can't communicate.

Where is the joy between us? What happened to our first bright rapport? Responsibilities must have crowded it out. It began to slip away so gradually we didn't even miss it. But I do miss it acutely at times. I grieve for it. And perhaps so does he.

So does he . . . God, thank you for that thought.

Bless my husband and let us find each other again. For his sake as well as mine let the ties of duty and habit be changed to something richer. For his sake as well as mine, drive out the devils of discontent.

Lord, bless this house and let me see its beauty even in disorder. Bless these children—their healthy bodies, their lively minds, their dearness. Bless my job. Let me be equal to it and fulfilled in it, or quit!

Above all, bless this family that you have put together in these surroundings for me to love and take care of.

Thank you that I can bring all this distress before you, God, and feel so healed and cleansed.

For Being Cherished

Lord, thank you for this simple yet priceless thing: Being cherished. For that old-fashioned word in old-fashioned wedding ceremonies, a word we take so for granted. Yet in reality how beautiful it is.

I'm untidy, my hair's a mess and so is the house. But the littlest fervently hugs my middle, and an eight-year-old presents me with a fragrant necklace of braided clover . . . A daughter banging in from school exclaims, "Hooray for anybody who can make gingerbread smell like that!" and gives me a kiss . . . My husband, toiling wearily in, perks up at sight of me and gives me another.

And suddenly, in a burst of awareness, I am overcome with this shining wonder: I am cherished!

I'm sick. Dizzy without warning. Trembling, not only with fatigue but a chill. Somebody says, "Go lie down, I'll finish the kitchen." I am being steered toward a hot bath, an already turned down bed. Cool hands are on my head.

I hear them making the phone calls I should be making, attending to things, sense their anxious tiptoeing about. And as I drift off there is something deeply sweet about even the misery that set all this in motion: I realize I am cherished.

We'll be late for the reception. As usual there's the last-minute search for the mislaid address; as usual I can't find my bag. And halfway down the block I set up a wail—a runner!

Patiently my husband turns back, waits with the motor running while I rush inside to change . . . And when I return, breathless, he leans over to pat my knee and say, "You're a lot of trouble, honey, but I guess you're worth it." And my heart leaps up in a little prayer of gratitude, God (I hope you hear it) just to thank you for being cherished.

Lord, you know how often I mourn for what I don't have: beauty or glamor or brilliance or money. You know how frequently I bewail our family's lacks and imperfections. Please cancel out all those complaints and make a note of this:

Even when I forget to say it, I do thank you day and night in my heart. For I know that I am one of the luckiest women in the world. A woman who is truly cherished.

The Flirt

Lord, look kindly upon this man who is a flirt. Don't let people judge him too harshly.

He smiles at women wherever he goes. He says flattering things to women. Sometimes he makes little passes at women. Yet I don't think he is truly a philanderer. I think he is merely a man who really admires and enjoys women—all sizes, kinds and shapes.

I know we are supposed to feel a little superior and contemptuous of men like that; the flirts are supposed to be compensating for something. And so a part of me is touched with a certain sympathy for him.

But I also *like* him, Lord. I think he is sometimes doing women a great kindness—to make even fat women, dull women, unattractive women feel, for a few moments, worthy of attention! Even a confirmed flirt can make a face light up, a whole being come alive under the rare treat of a man's admiration.

Bless him, Lord. Deal kindly with him. Don't let his motives be misunderstood.

The Generous Artistry

How generous is your artistry, God, that you made all things in creation to be enhanced by other things.

Leaves—how lovely in themselves.

How marvelous that they sprout like tiny parasols in the sweet spring air, are opened by the heat of summer, and turned from green to crimson and gold by the tangy chemistry of fall. But no, that is not enough. You have added the sun and the wind and the rain to toss them about, adorn them with bangles, make them dance and shimmer.

And the trunks of trees.

How stately they rise, strong and sufficient with their rough dark bark. They reach for the sky, making a mighty harmony of their own. Yet their beauty too must be heightened, given an added dimension by the silver brush strokes of sun and rain.

And the rain itself.

It is not just falling water to quench the thirst of the earth. It too is enhanced by all it touches—rooftops or leaves or lake. It runs across the water before the wind like an advancing army, shields flashing. Or it falls gracefully, each drop a dancer spreading her skirts on the shining surface of a ballroom floor.

Your rocks would not need to be embellished, God. Their gray-white stolidity, often glittering from their own white substance . . . their pure raw sculpturing. Yet even a rock is endlessly resculptured in sun and shadow and storm. Or a mantle of moss is tossed across its shoulders, or a meandering vine. Or flowers creep from a crevice. Or a bird's nest is tucked there, from which music spurts, and brisk bright wings.

For creatures too participate in this constant interplay of loveliness.

Dogs and cats and butterflies. Squirrels and people and children and all wild things. Life . . . life . . . all dipping and darting about together, or only just pausing to observe. But all adding myriad varieties of radiance and color.

How marvelous, this ever-changing pattern of the world's beauty, God. How you must love us to create for us such interlocking loveliness.

Don't let us ever be indifferent to it. Let us always see in it your generosity, your tremendous artistry.

"Pay Later"

Lord, please save them from their folly, these two who are so dear to me. They're about to tear their lives apart because of their problems about money.

Each year they've gone deeper into debt for things they thought they needed or just plain wanted. Buying each other expensive gifts, taking "pay later" trips, giving their children "advantages." "You only live once," they said, "and it's only money."

But somewhere along the line they *stopped* living, at least for each other. And began to exist only for the notes and mortgages and bill collectors. Now they're drowning in their sea of debt, and in their desperation blaming each other.

Even the extra jobs they've taken only pull them farther apart and add to the bitterness. They still love each other, but they don't think they can make it together any longer.

Please, Lord, save them from this mistake. Show them we can't solve financial problems by running away, we only compound them. Two households cost twice as much as one—and the children are bound to suffer.

If either of them were actually drowning, they would give their lives, if need be, to save each other. Lord, make them realize they must swim to each other's rescue now, with every ounce of strength and understanding. That together they can save their home and their love and their marriage.

Guide them to some practical solution, God. And oh, help all of us to remember that "pay later" all too often only means that we must pay *dearly* later.

Fortify Me with Memories

Sometimes life seems almost too wonderful, Lord.

My husband's arms around me. A new baby kitten-soft on my shoulder. A son who (after all that trouble) is turning into a bright and handsome boy. A daughter who's witty and lovely. A new puppy to be gathered around and adored.

Friends calling their good nights after an unusually happy party. A moment of rare understanding with another friend on the phone. An hour of high excitement when the mailman brings wonderful news.

There are times when all these things seem to shout and sing within me, Lord. To merge into something almost too beautiful, like a sunset or a symphony. Fused into some instant or hour of perfection. At times I can scarcely bear it, Lord—this beauty, this benediction.

Oh, help me to remember it, please . . .

When the baby screams all night with the colic. When the pup throws up on the kitchen floor. When my husband is cross and discouraged. When the son fails me and the daughter becomes a blind fury against me.

Gird me with the shining moments, God. Fortify me with memories.

Help me to realize during the pain and the petulance and the anguish that life *is* truly wonderful, Lord. And it takes the grim moments to enhance the ecstasy.

For Somebody Else

Lord, please let no day pass without my being nice to somebody. Doing a little extra for somebody that I don't have to.

Let me smile at a stranger or pay an unexpected compliment. Let me thank a clerk or a waitress who's done a good job. Let me wave a car ahead of me in traffic. Let me write a note of appreciation, hand a flower to a passing child, invite a hot and thirsty deliveryman to have a cold drink.

Let me run an errand for somebody, share my surplus with somebody, whether it be clothes or money or health and strength. Let me call on somebody who's lonely, or at least pick up the phone and say, "Let's talk."

Thank you, Lord, that the list is so long, the cost so little, and the opportunities every single day so great.

"Inasmuch as you have done it unto one of the least of these, my brethren," you once said, "you have done it unto me." Perhaps that's why there is such a sense of blessing in doing even little things we don't have to for somebody else.

Friends Are Worth Forgiving

Thank you, God, for showing me that friends are worth forgiving.

You know how hurt I've been by my dearest friend. I was so upset I thought, "I never want to see her again." But I did want to see her. Even as I nursed my wound I missed the things we've shared so long:

Our luncheon dates, our shopping trips, the nutty things we laugh about. Our confidences, our hopes, our long soul-searching conversations. She adds a dimension of joy and understanding to my life that I'd be lost without.

Thank you that I prayed about this, God. Even if at first I asked only that she apologize, admit she's wrong. For as I prayed, that part stopped seeming so important! It occurred to me how many faults I have, how many times I've probably offended—not only her but other friends—and been forgiven. And how bleak and empty the years would be if people hung onto their grievances instead of each other.

It came to me so clearly: *Friends are worth forgiving.*

So thank you that I pocketed my pride and called her and she sounded so glad to hear from me. (She's missed me too, I know. She's been as miserable as I've been.)

Right now my heart is singing for she's invited me over; we won't even mention what happened, we'll take up where we left off. I couldn't be happier if somebody had handed me a fortune.

A good friend *is* a fortune. A friend is worth forgiving.

Let Me Go Gently

Let me go gently through life, Lord, so much more gently.

Right now, calm my exasperation as I try for the third time to get that telephone operator to respond. Let me sit gently, think gently, speak gently when the connection is made. (It may not be her fault. Or she may be young and new to the job . . . or older and troubled by the very same problems I have.)

Smooth my sharp edges of person and temper and tongue. Give me gentleness in dealing with people. Strangers like this, who are human too, subject to error and hurt. And gentleness with my family . . . Not softness, no—keep me firm—but gentle of voice instead of shrill. Gentle of movement and manner and touch.

When life frustrates me, delays me, I want to grab it and shake it and rush it on. Or when it comes bashing and battering at me, every impulse yells, "Fight back!" But all this is so destructive, it only wastes more time and burns up precious energy. Remind me that true strengh lies in gentleness.

Help me to practice gentleness. In small inconveniences like this as well as large problems with those close to me. If I can just keep gentle, firm but gentle, then I'll be better able to meet life's major crises with dignity and strength.

Thank you for giving me gentleness, God.

The Courage to Be Kind

Dear Lord, give me . . . them . . . somebody the courage to be kind.

That poor man who just got on the subway is so shabby, so talkative, so obviously confused. He doesn't know where to get off, but the woman he asked just gave him a cold stare and pointedly moved away. The man on the other side of him has turned his back.

Nobody will help him, Lord, and my heart hurts. It hurts so for him, but it's pounding for me too. I don't want to be conspicuous—to have them stare coldly at *me*. But oh, Lord, I know where he wants to go, and I can't stand it any longer. Please give me the courage to lean across the aisle, force a smile and signal with my lips and my fingers: "Three more stops."

And now, oh, Lord, give me even more courage, for he has lurched over to my side. He wants to talk—talk in a loud, eager voice about the job he's going to apply for and why it's important that he get there on time.

Yes, yes, he's been drinking, and he probably won't get it, poor guy. But thank you that I'm able to listen, to offer a little encouragement and to see that he doesn't miss his stop.

Thank you for his grateful handclasp at parting, his smile from the platform, his jaunty yet wistful wave. Thank you that I no longer care what the other passengers think, because my conscience is at rest and my heart is warm.

Please help him, Lord, and bless him. And thank you for giving me the simple courage to be kind.

Let Me Raise My Own Children

Lord, help me to remember that nobody else can raise my children. Not neighbors or maids or baby sitters. Not schools nor even churches, important as they are. Not Scouts or Campfire Girls or Little Leagues or Y's. Not doctors or counselors or choir directors. Not music or dancing teachers. Not a hundred and one other people to whom so many of us entrust our offspring so many of their waking hours.

I am sometimes bewildered by all this army of other people, Lord. Good people, wise people, specialists many of them. Often I'm grateful; but often I feel a little guilty and concerned about them too. It's all too tempting to depend on them. To shoo the kids off to them thinking, "Good. You'll teach them, guide them, keep them busy, make them happy—I don't need to worry."

Besides, I've got so much else to do. Important things too—for the church, the community, my husband. Clubs and meetings to attend (some of them having to do with children). And there's our social life, our trips and entertaining. And the experts say I mustn't forget myself; I must feel free to study, take a job if I want to, express myself. The family's better off, they say, if you don't live just for them.

Sometimes I get very mixed up about all this, God. A deep, nagging voice insists that nothing is more important than raising my own children. In the only place they *can* be truly raised, their home. This house, these rooms, at their own table, with both parents present as often as humanly possible. Where else can they learn their manners or how to talk to each other, or the lessons of consideration and truth and love? Who else, however dedicated, can possibly *care* as much as we do whether they learn these lessons and what kind of people they become?

The years of their growing up are so precious, Lord, and so fleeting. Don't let me duck the responsibility you gave me along with the children. Help us all to sort out our priorities and to drop any activities that separate this family instead of uniting it.

Give me a firm new grip on the challenge of raising my own children, God—and a proud new joy in it.

New Day

Lord of this sun which I feel pouring in upon me at the beginning of this new day . . . Lord of the tree that I see swaying just beyond the window of this house . . . Lord of this house in which I live, and of all the years I have spent in it . . . Lord of the days I am yet to spend here, and of the next house to which I move . . . Lord of the eventual home you have prepared for me . . .

Bless this day I am about to begin.

Bless the work I will do in this place so that it will be productive for me and for others. Guide me so that I will use my time wisely. Direct me so that my energies will be spent most effectively.

Time is so precious; don't let me fritter it away on futile, silly things. Yet don't let me drive myself so hard that I don't enjoy it.

Whatever I do, whether large and seemingly important, or something so small as a phone call or making coffee, let it be vital, joyful, blessed with your presence. Enriched with your assurance that it is meaningful. That, however trivial, it really counts in the total scheme of a life composed of hours and days.

Thank you, God, for the marvel and the challenge of this new day.

Bless My Good Intentions

Lord, please bless my good intentions.

I make so many promises to myself about all the nice things I'm going to do: Have somebody over. Phone, write, send books and get-well cards and flowers.

You know how often I lie awake at night planning the delights I want to do for people. Or mentally writing the most beautiful letters.

You know my heart is full of love—but also how full of other things is my day. Duties, demands, problems. So that, all too often, these other things don't get past my mental gates. Or are hopelessly blocked or detoured when they do.

The get-well cards I buy get lost—or I can't find the right address. The people I try to cheer up with a phone call are already *on* the phone, or out! The budget won't quite stand the strain of flowers, and there's nothing but a few scraggly marigolds in the yard.

The cake I bake for the shut-in falls, or the car won't start to take it to her. When I sit down to write those lovely letters, the lovely words have vanished —or there's a sudden immediate crisis to be resolved.

They say hell is paved with good intentions, Lord. But I wonder if the paths to heaven aren't cobbled with them too?

Surely you give us credit for our kindly thoughts.

At least they're better than critical ones even when, through life's complications or our own procrastination, we fail to follow through.

You've shown us that we are more than body, we are spirit. And thoughts are powerful things. Maybe the vibrations of love they release, actually accomplish more than we know!

Anyway, Lord, please bless my good intentions.

Put My Worries to Work

Help me to be a better worrier, God. I don't agree with people who say worry is foolish and wrong and doesn't do any good. It's human to worry, it's natural, it's a by-product of caring, of love.

If I didn't worry about my husband's health, he'd never go to the doctor. Or worry about our son's grades, he'd never pass. If I didn't worry about even how this house looks, it would never get out of the mess it's so often in.

Thank you for these worries and the will to do something about them. Without some good old-fashioned worrying the world, and certainly this family, would go to pot.

But guard me against wasteful worrying. Futile mental wrestlings with things that can't be helped. (What a friend calls "The amputated limb.")

Some things cannot be changed: Mistakes of the past. Irreversible decisions. The afflictions over which we are powerless. . . . No, no, let me waste no worries on these. If I *must* worry, let it be for some good reason: my own reactions, how I will cope with what *is*.

Don't let me worry at night, Lord, when my body and mind need rest. Help me to herd all my worries into the daylight hours and to turn them over to you before I go to bed.

Let me do this in complete trust, knowing I'll be claimed by sleep—that precious sleep you gave us, not to be squandered in fruitless thought, but to replenish and strengthen us for all we must face by day.

Remind me, Lord, to follow my worries with action. No worry is worth the trouble if it doesn't spur me on to *do* something about the problem: To tackle it, challenge it, change it or forget it.

Help me to write that letter, make that phone call, have that confrontation, develop a plan to resolve whatever is troubling me.

Keep me from the habit of constant worry.

I realize that too much worrying bespeaks a lack of faith. But I think you gave us worry as a safeguard, God. A form of mental preparation. Of coming to grips with things.

When I must worry, then, help me put my worries to work, use them to some good purpose. Please make me a better worrier, God.

Hold Me Up a Little Longer

Hold me up a little longer, Lord, just a little longer.

I've been up since before daylight and it's so late and this P.T.A. speaker drones on and on. Just keep me awake until he stops (please make it soon) and revive me enough to help serve the doughnuts and coffee and get home.

The miles I've put on the car stretch behind me like a trip through eternity instead of a single day. To market and music lessons and the vet's. To the laundromat after our machine broke down. To the doctor's after our son got hit with a baseball bat. (Thank you, oh thank you that it wasn't serious, after all.)

What else, Lord? I'm too tired to remember. I just know that off somewhere there's a hot bath waiting. A bed waiting . . . my own dear sweet bed is waiting and the time will actually arrive when I'll sink gratefully into it . . . It will even be morning . . . tomorrow . . . next week!

Thank you for this image of respite, Lord. Of rest and energy renewed. Right now, this minute, prop me up, revive me.

Hang onto me just a little longer, Lord.

Why Won't They Listen to Me?

Why won't this family *listen* to me, Lord?

I don't mean my advice. They listen to that even if they don't take it—because it concerns *them*. But to me, just to me as a person.

They swarm around me with their demands. For food, fresh shirts, help with homework, sympathy, attention—the thousand things a mother isn't supposed ever to run out of. But even when they remember (on rare occasions) to thank me, it's as if they're blind and stone deaf to me.

Today I had a compliment I was dying to share, yes brag about. Forget it, nobody heard . . . And that conflict with the president of the club—a little moral support would have gone a long way, only I never got beyond telling them her name . . . Three times I tried to make somebody realize I had started reading a great new book they shouldn't miss . . . And that political argument at dinner—I could've straightened out a few things, maybe even won it, if they'd given me a chance to get *in*.

I hardly ever get to finish a sentence, Lord. They interrupt. They suddenly think of something they've got to do (or have me do for them). Or leave. It's as if a mother isn't supposed to have opinions or experiences or ideas that might just possibly be of interest to somebody. Her role is to be the perpetual wailing wall or cheering squad for everybody else.

* * *

I don't think this is fair, Lord. It makes me feel inadequate. Vacant in my head and heart. And, well —lonesome.

Is there something I can do to change their attitude? Yell? Demand attention? Take a course in public speaking? Or should I just accept it the way my mother had to, poor thing?

As . . . I suddenly realize—she *did!*

Dear Mother. I remember how she used to sigh: "My unfinished sentences are hanging all over this house." (Sentences that like everybody else, I helped to interrupt.)

A guilty amusement is beginning to work in me, Lord. Suddenly I feel better. Somehow I'm aware of all those unfinished sentences of my mother's dancing around like gay little garlands. Joining mine. Adorning me. Embracing me like her arms.

I can almost hear my mother laughing at my petulance. Telling me what I should have known all along: A family doesn't have to listen to a mother to love her. And isn't that all that really counts?

Don't Let Me Take It for Granted

Lord, don't let me take this wonderful gift of life for granted.

What a miracle it is just to wake up in the morning —to be alive another day!

Just to be able to get breakfast: to crack eggs into a sizzling skillet, to pour milk for the noisy horde. Just to feel myself *functioning*—muscles and mind and voice. (A voice the rest of the family probably wishes *didn't* work quite so well!)

Remind me to stop sometimes in the midst of it— the often chaotic, maddening midst of it—and touch it, taste it, love it, feel very grateful for it. Let my heart pause to utter a little secret prayer of thanks.

Lord, don't let me postpone my appreciation until all this may be threatened. Don't let me wait for a time when I might be ill—hurt, afflicted, in traction— and out of circulation before I realize it could be taken away.

Don't let me wait till it's over—as I know one day it will be—and I look back, perhaps alone. Don't let me wait till I'm desperate, Lord. Don't let me wait till I'm dying.

Help me to be fully awake and aware of the wonders of my life *now*, while I'm healthy and agile and able. Let me appreciate it while my family is all about me, in spite of the work and the worries they cause.

Let me keep my rejoicing current. As fresh as the eggs, as new as the morning paper, as bright as my children's faces or the sunlight dancing at the door.

Thank you for each day of our life together. Don't let me take it for granted.

Time Out for Love

Lord, don't ever let me be too busy to love . . .

A child who comes running in for a hug and lavish exclamations of praise because he's just learned to stand on his head. Yea, though I'm trying to make bouillabaisse and to keep the clams from getting all over the kitchen and the lobsters from crawling off, don't let me shoo him away.

Don't let me ever be too busy to love . . .

A neighbor who's just had a fight with her husband and needs a shoulder to cry on; or who's just had her first poem published and is dying to celebrate with someone. Though I'm already behind schedule and there's company coming, don't let me be too busy to listen and, in this way, to love.

Lord, don't let me be too busy to love . . .

A son who's home unexpectedly from boot camp with a buddy who hasn't got a home to go to—both starved for some good old-fashioned fried potatoes and corn bread. No matter how hectic my day's program, don't let me be too busy to fix it (well, at least give them a hand). Above all, to show him how thrilled I am to have him back and the other kid with him.

Don't let me be too busy to love, Lord . . .

My husband when he's tired and discouraged, or high from a big deal at the office, or simply wants my attention. Don't let me be too preoccupied with TV or a book or a friend on the phone or my own day's score of frustrations and peaks and valleys to give him what he longs for. Don't let me be too busy to love.

And now, Lord, thank you for giving me so many people, so many opportunities to love. But please forgive me when I fail them; help them to forgive me, and me to forgive myself.

You made me human, and there is only so much of me to go around.

Don't Let Her Hang onto Heartbreak

Help my friend to get over this tragedy, Lord. Don't let her keep hanging onto heartbreak.

Everyone pities her, but sorrow isn't a very congenial companion, and they're beginning to avoid her. She talks so much about it, dwells so on her memories she's actually nourishing her own pain.

By hanging onto heartbreak she's only making her own life lonelier.

Help her to snap out of it, Lord. To realize she's not the only one who's suffered a terrible loss. And that if everybody refused to say good-bye to grief, the world would be a dreadful place.

Give her the courage and the will to take up her old activities again. And to find some new ones among new people, especially people she can serve. Help her to heal herself through that greatest healing force of all, doing something for somebody else.

Some of the most radiant, gracious women I know have come through things like this, and worse. I know my friend can too if she'll just give up her dark affair with grief.

Stay very close to her, God. Bless her, love her, lead her to people who need her. Don't let her hang onto heartbreak.

These Conflicts About Children

Help us to resolve these conflicts about the children, Lord. These appalling differences about discipline and dating. About allowances, schoolwork. I think my husband is much too strict. He thinks *I'm* too lenient. And we're both so sure we're right.

Yesterday, for instance—I was shocked at the way he jumped our son about his grades. And last night, though I'd given our daughter permission, he said no, she could *not* go to the party after the football game.

We fought about it for hours. Knowing, even as we quarreled, that both of us want only what's best for the children. Because we *love* them. Almost as much as we love each other.

And that's the irony—that love should be so divisive. Love should mean union. Yet it's tearing us apart. Worse, it's tearing the children themselves in two.

God, forgive us. Give us the common sense and the will power not to argue or even discuss these issues before the children any more. And please show us a way to stop these conflicts.

Maybe, if my husband and I got away for a while, we could cease being adversaries and rediscover each other as people. Two people who do love each other. With a little peace and privacy we could pray about our differences. Not ask you to act as referee, but merely to show us what is truly best for these children you sent us, and how we can work together for them in harmony. As a team.

Meanwhile, Lord, I'm praying for that very thing. Help me to realize the first thing we've got to get rid of is the blind conviction we both have that we're always right.

Help me to remember that a man has experiences and insights that a woman may not comprehend, but that she'd better heed. And make my husband more aware of the values of *my* instincts and knowledge as a woman.

Surely, with a little patience and understanding, our separate natures can complement each other, Lord. So that the things that now divide us can actually draw us closer. And the love that was once strong enough to create the miracle of these lives, can unite us in a way that is just as wonderful, to give them the guidance they need.

Thank you for this revelation and this promise.

Possessions

Help me not to put too much stock in possessions, Lord. Mere possessions.

I want things, sure I want things. Life seems to be a continual round of wanting things, from the first toys we fight over as children, on through our thrilled counting of the wedding presents . . . Not primarily love and friends and pride in what we can do, but *things*.

Sometimes I'm ashamed of how much I want things. For my husband and the house and the children. Yes, and for myself. And this hunger is enhanced every time I turn on the TV or walk through a shopping mall. My senses are tormented by the dazzling world of *things*.

Lord, cool these fires of wanting. Help me to realize how futile is this passion for possession. Because— and this is what strips my values to the bone—one of my best friends died today in the very midst of her possessions.

The beautiful home she and her husband worked so hard to achieve, finally finished; furnished the way she wanted it, with the best of everything . . . The oriental rugs she was so proud of. The formal French sofas. The paintings. The china and glass and handsome silver service . . . She has been snatched away, while silently, almost cruelly, they remain.

Lord, I grieve for my friend. My heart hurts that she had so little time to enjoy her things. Things she had earned and that meant so much to her. But let me learn something from this loss:

That possessions are meant to enhance life, not to become the main focus of living. That we come into the world with nothing, we leave with nothing.

Help me not to put too much stock in mere possessions.

Nice Person

Please make me a nice person, Lord.

Not "nice" in the moral sense, important as that is. Not "nice," heaven forbid, in the sense of, "Be careful, she might be offended." But nice in the most human possible sense:

Nice for my husband and children to come home to. Nice for my friends. Somebody really nice to know.

But just as important as being nice to those dear to me, let me be nice to people whose lives even briefly touch mine. A waitress, a bus driver, a clerk. A child selling tickets to the Scout circus. A stranger asking directions. A peddler, a beggar; yes, even a panhandler or a poor drunk.

Don't let me ever be too much "a lady" to be kind.

You know I can't be perfect, Lord, but please put a smile on my face more often than a frown. Whatever else is wrong with me, let me at least be nice to look at for that reason.

And let me be nice to listen to. Keep the crossness out of my voice even when I'm tired and discouraged and the exasperations mount. Don't let me take my secret miseries out on other people. Let the music of my love for them sing a stronger song.

And let me be nice not only on the surface, Lord, but down—clear down. Genuinely interested in others. Concerned with their problems. Ready to help, to encourage, to go to bat for them. And so truly generous of spirit that their happiness and success is like my own.

Make me a nice person, Lord. And for the right reasons.

Not to be popular. Not to be loved. Not even to be liked. But because each step we take on the way to becoming a nice person is so rewarding, *feels* so good.

And though the way is hard and we often stumble, each step leads us a little closer both to happiness—and to you.

The Son Who Won't Study

Lord, help me to be more understanding of my children's limitations. Guard me against demanding more of them than they are equipped to give.

This son, so bright about anything mechanical, who's up half the night with his ham radio, and is always grubby from rebuilding cars. He's failing in school because he simply won't study. Except for motoring magazines, he won't even *read*.

You know how hard I've tried. Trips to the library, books of his own. I've nagged, scolded, coaxed, pleaded, threatened, offered rewards. And now that they say he's not going to pass, I've stormed.

I shudder at that memory, Lord. My yelling—and his furious, half-bitter, half-bewildered retorts. And that last accusation before he slammed off: "I can't help it, Mom. Stop trying to make me into something I'm not!"

Something he's not . . . and never will be. A professional man like his father. A lover of books and language like me . . . How much he'll *miss*, my very soul grieves. But am I grieving so much for him as for myself?

How can he "miss" something that's alien to his nature, that he's never enjoyed? Any more than I "miss" the things so vital to him? I'm lucky to get a car started, let alone cope with its insides. The very

idea of greasy engines is revolting to me . . . What if somebody tried to force me to build a radio?

Help me to see his side of it, Lord, as I sit now in what seems the wreckage of my dreams for my son—and yes, my pride. Help me not to consider what *I* want for him, but what *you* want for him. Since you made him so different from us you must have had your reasons. Help me to understand those reasons and release him to go his different way.

Maybe he's meant to go to trade school instead of high school or college. If so, let me remember how many bright and wonderful people have worked with their hands and haven't gone to college, and how much they've done for the world.

Dear Lord, instead of bemoaning my son's lacks, let me be grateful for his accomplishments. His excellent mind that comprehends things I can't. His skillful hands. Thank you for these gifts, God. Give me new pride in them, and help me to convey that pride to him.

I now accept my son for what he is and can be. I affirm and claim a happy, productive life for him.

The Extra Measure of Strength

Lord, you know I've just about had it. Up night after night with the children—sick ones, scared ones, the ones who've wet their beds. And no time to catch up on my rest by day.

And all the problems. Financial problems, emotional ones.

I feel near the point of exhaustion. Yet I know that if I keep near to you I won't quite collapse.

Thank you for giving me that little extra measure of strength I need to get through each night, each day.

Right now, that's all I ask.

The Healing

Thank you, Lord, that tonight my heart is light. Like something newly freed. For I have discovered how to heal it of an unexpected wound; one of those slight, seemingly small rebuffs or humiliations or blows that ought not to hurt so much, but for some of us who are unduly sensitive maybe, they do: A bawling out from the boss. A scolding from someone dear. A sharp word from a friend. Even rudeness from a stranger.

Such things can strike the sunshine from the day. The spirit winces, beats a quick retreat. We feel our wet eyes sting.

Then pride urges retaliation. Sometimes we want to turn on somebody else, as if to pass the pain along. Only now, Lord, I know the true way to relief is to cancel out the pain by doing something kind.

Thank you that today, still seething and suffering, I found myself seated on a bus beside a small shabby man. And I realized, as he stared fixedly out the window, that he was struggling not to cry. And my own little hurt seemed to shrink before the enormity of his. I knew I must speak to him—and did.

And he turned to me, Lord, and drew from his threadbare wallet a picture of a bright-eyed little girl six years old. "We lost her yesterday," he said. He was going now to pick out flowers. He wanted to talk about it. He was glad somebody cared. In our few blocks' ride across the city we shared it—his pride in her and his great loss.

And we touched upon the mystery of being born at all, of being parents, of the brevity and beauty of life upon your earth. And when we parted he was actually smiling. "You've made me feel so much better," he said.

"You've made me feel better too," I told him. For my own petty pain no longer mattered. It was as if some balance had been struck between that which is hurtful and that which is healing.

And perhaps that is all that really matters. That the good, the kind, the decent in this world can equal and even surpass the bad.

Thank you that I have learned this lesson, Lord. Next time it surely won't be so hard to overcome an unexpected hurt.

Doormat Mother

God, help me to stop being such a martyr. Such a doormat mother.

Nobody thanks me for it. Nobody even *wants* me to be. Yet I've given in so much, given up so much, allowed myself to be inconvenienced and overworked so much that I've slipped into a dark insidious love affair with hurt.

I'm beginning to crave it, Lord, I'd rather be hurt than happy!

When there's a conflict over the car I say, "Go on, I'll manage." Feeling noble and abused as I take a bus or call a cab, wanting them to feel sorry. Or I even stay home, wallowing in misery.

I find myself slaving over dinner or cleaning up afterward, hurt that nobody offers to help, but too proud or long-suffering to ask. Paying myself off in self-pity.

Last year when people forgot my birthday I *was* hurt, deeply. But this year I was almost hoping to be hurt, I was a little disappointed when they all remembered. The other night I was prepared to be lonely and hurt because everybody was going to the beach, I thought, without me. When they urged me to come too I felt almost cheated.

Oh Lord, heal me of this sick need to be stepped on, neglected, wounded. Restore to me a lively, healthy self-respect. How can other people stand me if I think so little of myself that I don't expect to be treated well?

Help me to realize that to sacrifice yourself for others without being glad about it is no sacrifice at all. "The gift without the giver." And a gift that imposes chains of guilt. Help me to free myself—and my family of the shackles of my martyrdom.

Don't let me be selfish, God, but don't let me be such a doormat either. Give me the poise and the cheer and the self-respect just to be a good mother!

Let Them Remember Laughter

Lord, whatever else my family remembers of me (the mistakes, the tears, the temper) please let them also remember my laughter. Guard me against ever becoming a grim and cheerless mother unable to see the funny side, even when things go wrong.

Lord, keep my laughter especially on tap when I'm the culprit in the case: When I've locked us all out of the house or the car . . . When my lovingly molded mousse skids onto the kitchen floor . . . When I've pulled some awful boo-boo with the president of the P.T.A. or the grande dame of the neighborhood . . . When I've dyed my hair the wrong color, or ruined a dress I was making, or gotten us all hopelessly entangled in wet wallpaper . . . help me to see the comedy of my errors.

Instead of stamping and storming, let me give my children the healing gift of laughter.

Lord, let me be a mother who can laugh with her children.

Don't let me ever laugh *at* them when they're trying to please me, no. Never when they're awkward, discouraged or troubled. But remind me to laugh more freely, gaily at their antics and their stories. Yea, though I've witnessed such clowning so often, heard the same jokes before, equip me with patience and a convincing show of enthusiasm. They need an audience so much.

Let me applaud with my heart as well as my hands. Help me to give them the sweet gift of laughter.

The same thing goes for my husband, God.

He needs an audience too, he needs a cheering section (and goodness knows after all these years *his* comedy routines are familiar). But mainly let him remember me as laughing more often than crying the blues.

I know that a family means problems, Lord. A family means troubles large and small. Troubles I can't always expect to "come smiling through." But with your help no troubles can overcome us, and laughter helps too.

Lord, let no day pass that my family doesn't hear my laughter.

A Prayer for Boys

Thank you, God, for boys.

Little boys and big boys, and yes, that overgrown boy I sometimes see in the man I married.

Please keep my mind from criticizing them so often, my tongue from being so quick to scold them.

Give me the patience to listen to them. The wisdom to understand them. The spirit and humor to laugh with them. And the strength sometimes to endure them.

Give me the courage to differ with them and discipline them when I have to. But make me the kind of woman who can comfort them, help them, encourage them. Maybe even inspire them.

Above all, show me how to enjoy them—for only then can they be happy and enjoy themselves.

Thank you for them, God, and help me take good care of them.

God bless boys.

An Instrument of Peace

"Make me an instrument of thy peace," prayed St. Francis of Assisi. And I sometimes wonder if he shouldn't have been a woman, Lord. For surely only a mother can truly appreciate that prayer.

I utter it every day as I try to smooth ruffled feathers, assuage hurt feelings, bring understanding between brothers and sisters, husband and children. As I strive to explain different people's viewpoints to each other (without at the same time betraying confidences)—*peace, oh let there be peace!*

You hear me praying it, almost without thinking, as I portion out money or cookies or my own attention; as I maneuver arrangements about belongings—skates and skis and sweaters, and turns—who's to have a slumber party, who's to take the car: *Give me the wisdom to be fair, give us peace.*

And how hopefully I pray it, scheming to concoct meals that will be conducive to cheerful conversation instead of arguments. And how fervently I pray it, steering that conversation to quieter waters if it threatens to get out of hand.

I sometimes wonder if we're failing as parents, Lord, that this has to be my continual prayer? But surely it's just because we're raising human beings; and there are bound to be conflicts whenever people live under one roof. And the stronger the ties of love and blood, the stronger these conflicts sometimes are.

So keep right on making me an instrument of thy peace. Not always as strong and sharp and shining as I'd like, not nearly as perfect (often rusty and blunted and useless, I fear) but an instrument, nonetheless.

Thank you that St. Francis gave mothers the perfect prayer.

The Gossip

What do I do about this woman who is such a gossip, God?

She's really a very good woman underneath that lively tongue. She's always doing things for people, calling on the sick, sending over casseroles and fresh bread, letting the kids build forts in her yard. And she's done me so many favors, driven me to market, lent me her silver coffee service, gotten me into her club.

But when she calls or I see her coming, part of me winces—part of me can hardly wait. Because now I'll get the lowdown on the whole neighborhood. (My husband calls her the Town Crier.) And so much of it is the negative, the juicy stories:

Who's about to be divorced or getting fired. Who's having a baby—usually minus marriage or too soon. Who got drunk or smoked pot at a party. Why that police car was parked so long down the block. True, she does occasionally pass on good news too—somebody's promotion, somebody's recovery or coming trip to Europe. (As I said, she's not malicious, more just *curious*, and a born reporter.) But it's really the dirt she gets the most kick out of conveying, and makes the most exciting.

She hasn't got anything juicy to spread about us (at least not yet!) so I'm not scared of her, God. I'm scared about—me. Because even if I don't join in (well, not too much) I'm tempted. I'm dying to tell her all the negative stuff I know or suspect, and after she's gone there is the temptation to pass on what she's told me.

This kind of gossip is contagious, Lord, and I've discovered I'm not immune!

The innocent gossip I don't worry about, the kind that's born of a healthy normal interest in people and what they're doing. Yet this other kind of gossip—I know it can cause harm, I know it's wrong. So even if I can't hope to cure her, I've got to learn how to steer her back to the other kind—and have the will power to try.

Please give me the courage and moral strength to do this, Lord. And fortify me with love. I don't want to hurt her feelings.

She's really a wonderful woman. (And she does make wonderful bread.)

You Can't Have Everything

I thought this woman had everything, Lord: The perfect house, the perfect children, the perfect marriage. Even the perfect career. I used to envy her, however I tried not to.

I used to come home from a party where she and her husband had danced so beautifully together, seemed so much in love . . . or from their home where everything was so exquisite . . . or the school where their son got all the honors . . . or the studio where her paintings had been on exhibit—and feel a pang of resentment.

"Life's so unfair," I used to think. "Why should one person have so much?"

But now I'm shocked to discover that nobody, not even this woman, has everything.

That behind that perfect marriage, the walls of that perfect house, have been problems and agonies nobody suspected. Her husband is an alcoholic—they've been hiding it for years. Their son, that perfect son, got into trouble and has disappeared. Their daughter has leukemia—she may not live . . . Things this woman has endured in silence, been too proud or courageous to reveal!

And oh, Lord, I'm so ashamed of the moments of jealousy I felt. My heart is heavy with guilt; my whole being aches for her. Please bless and help her, this woman I thought had everything. Put your arms around her family. And show me how, without intruding, I can help them.

And whenever I'm tempted to compare my lot with others, let me remember that appearances can be deceiving. Each life has its drawbacks and its burdens. Lord, don't let me ever forget: nobody has everything.

Getting at It

Oh, Lord, please help me to stop worrying about this annual bazaar they've put me in charge of, and get *at* it!

You know how weak I am, and what a procrastinator. How I let myself get talked into things I sometimes later regret. How I lie awake nights dreading what I've undertaken, scared I won't be up to it. You know the times I've panicked, even considered making excuses for myself and trying to get out of it.

And the longer I put off getting started the worse it gets.

Now, with your help, this is going to stop. Not only because time's flying by and there's so much to be done, but because I'm ashamed of this self-inflicted suffering.

So here goes, God. Today, this minute, I'm getting at it. (There. The very resolution has a calming effect!)

I'm drawing up a plan of action. I'm calling committee meetings. I'm already getting ideas, exciting ones (what strange things happen once the gates are simply unlocked)!

I know it won't be easy; but you've made me realize it won't be all that hard. You will give me self-confidence and strength—and ultimate success. But you can't do any of these things for any of us until we *start*.

* * *

(Come to think of it—if you created the world and its creatures and even the universe in seven days, you must have just made up your mind and *done* it. And maybe even *you* didn't realize how great was your own potential or how vast would be the result.)

Let Me Take Time for Beauty

Lord, let me take time for beauty.

Time for a jug of flowers on the table, or a plant if flowers aren't in bloom. Time for a dab of lipstick or a fresh blouse before the family comes home. Don't let me settle for the dingy, the shabby, the ugly—either with myself or with my house, just because I'm too lazy to make the effort.

Give me the energy and the will to provide a bit of beauty.

You've made the world so beautiful, Lord, let me take time to see it. Even as I'm rushing to the market or driving children to their destinations, let me be aware of it: the glory of hills and woods and shining water. The colors of traffic lights and yellow buses, of fruit stands and lumberyards, of girls wearing bright scarves that dance in the breeze.

Let me take time for the beauty in my own back yard, Lord.

Let me lift my eyes from the dishes to rejoice in the sunshine spilling through the trees. In the squirrels darting jaunty-plumed along the bleached boards of the fence. In the raindrops strung out on the clothesline like a string of crystal beads.

Let me take time for the children. How quick they are to discover beauty and come running to us with their offerings.

Don't let me be too busy to exclaim over these treasures: a bluejay's bright feather, the first violets and dandelions, a shell, a pretty stone. God, forgive me for the time (I wince to remember) when, involved in some dull task—ironing maybe—I shooed away a child who was begging, "Look, come look. A butterfly!" A cocoon was breaking, I learned later. He wanted me beside him to witness this miracle, this birth of beauty out of its dark cage.

Dear God, to live at all is such a miracle—whether as bug or bird or creature of any kind. To come into existence upon this planet and be able to witness its beauty is such a privilege, especially for a human being.

Help us to cherish and be a part of that beauty.

Let me take time for beauty, God.

The Quarrel

We quarreled last night, Lord, and I'm sure the children heard.

They looked so self-conscious this morning. Our daughter's eyes were stricken. And our son was so abrupt at breakfast; he barely said good-bye before rushing off for school . . . Even the littlest held me too close before going out to play. Even she sensed something wrong; her small innocent face was puzzled.

Forgive me, God. Forgive us both. Because now our differences are over (well—almost over). We'll soon forget—but will they? The things we said to each other really don't hurt us as much as I'm afraid our words hurt *them*.

Lord, please help us to show our children that even though we fight sometimes, we really do love each other. That their home is safe and our differences have nothing to do with them.

I'm going to run into my husband's arms tonight when he comes home from the office. I'm going to be especially cheerful and see that dinner is especially good . . . He'll respond, I know he'll respond, and so will they.

Thank you, Lord, that you always give us a chance to make up, right wrongs. And though we're not perfect and will probably fight again, please help us not to fight very often. And meanwhile, every day of our lives, to prove to our children how deeply we care about each other and the home we are making for them.

This House to Keep

Sometimes my home just seems so cozy, God. For no special reason it suddenly seems warm and dear— as if it had put sheltering arms around me. I feel snug, protected, like a mole deep in its burrow, or a bird in its nest.

This kitchen with its clutter . . . This bedroom with its tumbled beds . . . The family room, deserted now but warm with the memories of last night's music, last night's fire.

I feel shielded by these walls, and yet in charge. So joyfully in charge. They are mine, to do with what I please. I want to spread my wings, to draw them a little closer to my heart.

Deep instincts stir. Half-buried recollections . . .

Of childhood playhouses of the past . . . In a garage. Under the attic eaves. Or down in the ravine, with tall ferns for curtains, and fallen logs and rocks for furnishings. How snug and secret it felt and yet how free, especially when raindrops spattered overhead.

You know, Lord, how often I hate this house. Mourn its defects, deplore its confusion, want to flee its confining walls. Yet on some days love rises up to compensate—like the guilty, almost overpowering love I feel when I've been cross or unfair to the children. I want to hug it as I do them, to wash its face, straighten its clothes, tuck it in. To make it as clean and sweet and charming as I possibly can.

Because it's a part of my life, even as they are. It echoes my tastes, reflects my character, and for all its imperfections, it is warm and dear to me.

Thank you, Lord, that I have this house to keep.

Psalm for Deliverance

I pleaded with God to deliver me from this trouble.

My brain was bruised from seeking solutions. My body ached from the effort. My nerves were strung tight; they would break, I knew, something would break if I forced myself to go on.

"Help me," I kept crying. "Give me answers. Deliver me from this torment." But my own voice seemed to despair of such deliverance even as I called.

Then a strange quiet came upon me. A kind of divine indifference. I knew without words or even thoughts that I need only withdraw and wait quietly upon the Lord.

And he did not forsake me.

He came in the quiet of the night. He was there in the brilliance of the morning. He touched my senses with hope, he healed my despair. And with the awareness of his presence came the deliverance I sought.

The answers would be provided. Quietly, and in God's own way, they were working even as I waited.

Don't Let Me Stop Growing

Don't let me ever stop growing, God. Mentally growing.

This mind you have given me (any mind!) has such marvelous potential. Why should I hobble it to a house, shackle it to a kitchen sink, cuddle down with it behind a coffee clache?

It's tempting, Lord, and all too easy to give up, make excuses, do the most comfortable thing. To settle for small talk, small interests, small horizons. I've seen this happen to so many women, some of my brightest friends. No wonder they're bored, God. Restless and bored. And boring.

Don't let this happen to me. Let me learn at least one new thing about something important every day. (Well, at least every other day.) Let no day pass without reading. Keep my mind always open, lively, reaching out for new interests, new knowledge.

Don't let me stop mentally growing.

Keep me always growing, God. Emotionally growing.

Help me outgrow my tears, my sometimes childish tantrums. The periods of self-pity when I tell myself nobody loves me, like I used to as a little girl. Please rescue me whenever I revert; steer me firmly forward into the calm waters of mature behavior. Let me feel the thrill of self-command, the dignity of self-control.

I want to keep emotionally growing.

*   *   *

Help me to keep growing, God, in relation to others.

So many people need me, depend on me, look to me for help, for answers. And I so often feel inadequate, unequal to their demands. Sometimes I even feel impatient and resentful, not wanting to be bothered. (Why should they drain my time and energy?) Forgive me for this feeling, Lord, and fortify my reserves.

Broaden my understanding. Deepen my compassion. Give me more wisdom and joy in sharing when I can.

As a wife, mother or friend, help me to keep growing.

Don't let me ever stop growing, God. Spiritually growing. Drawing ever closer to you, the source of it all: The universe. The world and the life upon it. The people ... the person ... myself.

I want to know you better, tune in more truly with the harmonies of all your creation, including the life that is my own.

Thank you for this person that you made in your image, Lord. Don't let me ever stop growing.

The Chain of Hands

Lord, what a wonderful thing it is that your people can help each other.

I think sometimes of all the people who have helped me. Where would I be without the ones who helped by giving me jobs, who helped me go to the college? And the wonderful teachers there who did so much to help and encourage me.

And the people who helped after marriage. The doctors and ministers and friends and family and neighbors. Yes, and strangers. People who kept the children, lent me things, gave me things, told me things, put themselves out, went to bat for me. All of it free, gratis. With no expectation of favors returned.

Lord, I would feel forever in debt if it weren't for the warm comforting feeling of knowing I too have helped others. That there are people in this world whose lives are a bit easier, who wouldn't be where they are either, if it hadn't been for me.

This chain of human beings so willing to hold out their hands to each other—how it must please you. Partly because it pleases us so much.

And although the hand we extend to help someone, and the hand that receives it, may never touch again —yet the help goes on. The scales balance. Somewhere, someday that other hand will reach out to smooth the way for somebody else.

Lord, don't let me ever forget those who have given me a lift along the way. And let no day pass that I don't help somebody else—if only to repay those who have helped me.

The Good Neighbor

Help me to be a better neighbor, Lord.

Don't let me be too busy to welcome the new family, or to drop in on that lonely soul down the street.

Make me the kind of neighbor people can borrow from if they have to, or who can be counted on to bring in the mail, keep an eye on a child, or to give somebody a lift.

Keep me from being a nuisance neighbor, Lord, don't let me ever intrude. But let me be ready to help and comfort any neighbor in need.

Lord, help me to be an understanding neighbor.

When it comes to other people's yards and parties, and dogs and cats and kids—curb my complaints. Remind me always to live and let live.

Above all, help me not to judge. Lock the gates of my mind against envy and suspicion. Guard my tongue from gossip. Don't let me criticize my neighbors—not unless I'm willing to have my own faults weighed in the same scales.

Make me a cheerful, friendly neighbor. Someone who speaks to everybody, quick to call a greeting that might brighten somebody's day.

And make me a kind neighbor. As nice to the paperboy or the Brownie Scout selling cooking as to the president of the Garden Club.

Make me a hospitable neighbor. Ready with a cold drink, a cup of hot coffee, an extra plate on the table. And as willing to entertain as I am to be entertained.

Let the *Welcome* on our doormat mean exactly what it proclaims.

Help me to be a better neighbor, Lord, even though I know I can't live up to all these things.

Life is so hectic for us. I am so busy, most people today are so busy. And today people come and go. We simply don't have time or opportunity to "neighbor" in the old-fashioned sense when families lived side by side for years.

Yet people still need each other. Neighbors still need each other. Thank you for the wonderful neighbors I have, Lord. And help me to be a better neighbor.

Generous Measure

Dear Lord, where does all this stuff come from?

These objects nobody seems to use any more. Toys, tennis rackets, toasters, tools, suitcases, pans. These clothes that crowd the closets. I just get the cupboards and closets cleaned, winnowed out, the trucks haul things away (Good Will, American Rescue, Salvation Army—such cheerful names, so appropriate to my dilemma) and they're full again.

I get a little tired of it, Lord, a little cross.

Then I smile as the words from the Bible come winging through my consciousness: "And I shall give you good measure, pressed down and running over."

Running over is right! The whole place is always running over—including the attic, the basement, the garage. You have blessed us far over and beyond what we need or deserve. And instead of fussing about this abundance, I should be thankful. And I am. Believe me, Lord, I'm grateful.

(But sometimes I am also almost tempted to ask . . . hold off a little, will you?)

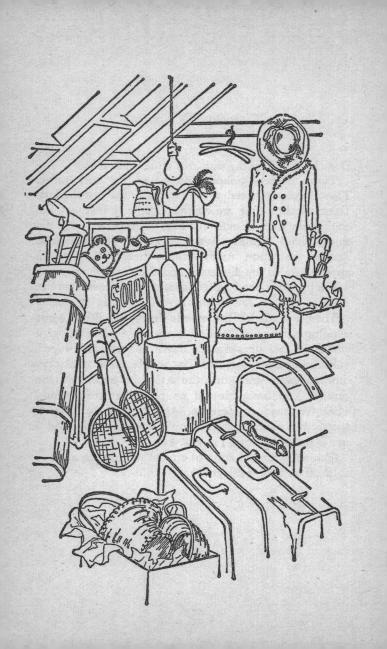

Bless All These Losses

These losses, Lord, all these losses. Why do I have these spells of *losing* things?

Last week my glasses. My wallet the week before. (Thank you that whoever found it at least had the decency to return my credit cards.) And now this— my favorite sweater. That beautiful cable-knit. The last thing my grandmother made for me. I remember taking it off on the bus (how could I have been so careless?) but don't remember having it at the picnic. But I've called and called, and people have searched and searched. Now I know with a sense of despair and dismay, that I'll never see that lovely thing again. It's gone.

I could cry—and have. I could berate myself—and do. I could get mad at the fate that seems to dog me. Lost car keys, books, umbrellas, letters. But I know that simply blaming fate or even myself too much doesn't do any good. I've got to accept this loss as gracefully as I can. And bless it! Yes, bless it to some good purpose so that it won't *be* total loss.

Lord, please let whoever found that sweater be someone who really needs a sweater. Let it be some- body who might otherwise be cold. Let my sweater keep that person warm. And may its lovely colors add a little joy and beauty to that life as well.

And likewise bless all my trivial losses. The books I lose—let them speak to other minds when they are found, let them be read. And the umbrellas—let them shelter somebody else from the storm.

(I don't know just how to bless my glasses or the car keys or the mail, but maybe I needed the setbacks and consternation that losing them brought.)

Anyway, Lord, as I bless these foolish losses, let me remember how small they really are in the total scheme of things. Thank you that I've lost only a sweater—even Grandmother's lovely sweater—and not a husband . . . a child . . . a friend.

Let Them Join in My Rejoicing

Lord, help me to bear witness to the wonders of life more often. When I'm happy, remind me to say so.

I'm vocal enough about my problems, prompt to proclaim the fact when things go wrong. Why doesn't it occur to me to rejoice and give thanks not only to you but to others—particularly my family—when things go *right*?

These children, so often a worry. The budget, so often strained. Neighbors and friends sometimes a nuisance instead of a joy. My own personal plans so often thwarted, my disappointments so often plain.

Now and then I come up short to realize I must project the image of a person forlorn! When actually —you know it, God, and *I* know it—I feel very lucky in my lot, and most of the time contented.

Why then am I afraid to let others know it? Outsiders—yes, one must be careful with outsiders. When a woman starts proclaiming "I'm happy, everything's great!" people are liable to think she's bragging, or merely putting up a front. But even with my friends, Lord, those who really know me, help me to affirm the values of life more often than I indulge in hand-wringing.

As for the family—why are so many of us prone to keep our happiness a secret when it would mean so much to them?

Is it that we're leery of tempting fate? Fearful that today's exulting may become tomorrow's anguish? As well it might. Yet the very prospect of troubles unsuspected ought to make our hosannas louder on the days when we can sing.

Or is there a little bit of the martyr in every mother? Are we reluctant to admit our pleasure lest people fail to appreciate all we do for them?

Whatever it is, help me to banish these foolish barriers. Let me fling wide the gates to my private garden of happiness, and bid those who are so dear to me come in.

The Answer Tree

I sometimes wish I had an answer tree, God. A tree that I could shake and have answers come raining down like apples. Answers to everybody's questions, the family's and my own:

Answers about schools and friends and money and problems of the heart. About what's safe and what isn't, what's right and what's wrong. Answers to specific things like math and wind and weather and how a rocket can hurl men to the moon. Answers to complex things like drugs and sex and religion and marriage.

I have to search so deeply into my own being for the answers, Lord—my experience, my concepts, my training. And groping, probing, producing what I can only hope are the right answers, I often feel so unequal to the responsibility imposed. I long to just reach up beyond myself to some sturdy, dependable tree of correct answers, give it a shake and hold out my hand.

Then I realize that wouldn't really be very interesting. I kind of enjoy being considered a human computer spewing out solutions. Even when I have to admit, "I don't know," or urge, "Stop depending on me, make up your own mind," there is something dear about the role. And life would be lacking without the mystery, the suspense of never knowing for sure whether you've given the right advice.

Besides, I have you to help me. In talking things over with you I become secure. You are the source of the answers. You help lead me to the right decisions.

Thank you that mothers can't just shake an answer tree. Prayer is even better. We know that if we turn to you in trust we will be given the answers. (And it gives us a chance to ask somebody else!)

The Wonder of Being One

Lord, thank you for the growing awareness that all of us are truly one. This sense of identity with other people—suddenly, only today, you sent it newly singing through my consciousness.

That little lost boy in the store, running about like a wild thing, screaming for his mother. When I caught him and tried to comfort him, I could feel his small heart beating, his tears were wet on my cheek. And when at last his mother came rushing up, the three of us held each other, our tears mingling, and the revelation swept through me—there is no difference! We are one.

They are of a different race, Lord, a different culture. We could communicate only with our bodies and our eyes. Yet flesh is the same, feelings of fear and love and rejoicing are the same. You made us one.

I walked on through that crowded store with new eyes, Lord. An old man limping ahead of me, obviously weary, with feet that hurt. My own feet and back have hurt often enough to merge with his misery, perhaps ease it a trifle with a smile of understanding. Anyway, my heart sent out its newfound message: It's not just you. And age or sex don't matter. We are one!

A teen-ager struggling through the revolving door with her packages . . . They spilled onto the street, and helping her retrieve them, we both laughed. I was a clumsy, apologetic girl again—and every woman who had ever given me a hand. She and I were simply female. One.

Driving home through the traffic . . . All the faces beside me in the lanes. Men, looking tired or worried, heading for their families in the suburbs. Carpools of joking co-workers. A Girl Scout leader whose station wagon swarmed with green uniformed shriekers.

She and I exchanged bemused, commiserating glances that said, "You just have to bear up, don't you?" For in that moment of unspoken communion we were one.

Thank you for this day's experiences that make me realize we are all little fragments of you, God. We are all just visibly separate particles of your love. You have made us in different shapes and sizes and colors, given us different roles to play in our various adventures upon this earth. Yet flowing through us all is the self-same current of life and human emotion that merges us one with another. And with you.

Knowing this, how can we hurt each other or try to subtract from each other? God, help us always to give to each other, so that we may grow in the wonder of being one.

Forgiving Means Forgetting

I don't find it too hard to forgive, Lord—what's hard is to forget.

When someone is truly sorry I think, "Yes, yes, I forgive you." Just to have the estrangement over, to be relieved of the awful pain of being parted even mentally from someone I love. In sheer self-protection I think I "forgive."

But the memory remains. Deep, buried deep inside me, the deed or the word still lives. And it rises sometimes to taunt me, to wreck the peace I've achieved.

Why, Lord? Why do these memories linger?

Is it because I've forgiven for the wrong reasons? Selfish reasons. Not genuine compassion and love and charity for the other person and his human frailties, but for myself. Me—me—*me.* Because I can't stand to be so hurt.

Help me to change this, Lord. Make me strong enough to forgive people out of love rather than a mere frantic desire to ease my own wounds. Forgive so wholly, fully, in such a flood there is no room for nagging memories.

Thank you for teaching me to forgive this way. True forgiving means forgetting.

Needlework Prayer

Thank you for the joy of needlework, Lord. Though I sometimes wonder why I do it. All this time and money to fashion something I could buy far more easily . . . A canvas already painted, an already-woven cover or cushion or rug.

Yet here I sit persevering, inching toward the dream. Drawing these strands of color in and out, watching my own living fingers create the scene.

What deep secret drive impels me, Lord? So that I keep returning to my task, and when it is finished begin anew.

A love of beauty, yes, and the thrill of creating beautiful things. But more. For as I stitch away I feel *in* love, not only with this, my chosen pattern, but people too. My family, my friends, those who will eventually see this work and perhaps love it as well. But in a deeper sense—I love you.

I think of you whose canvas is the universe, and how tirelessly you make it beautiful for us. How you needlepoint the sky with stars, and cover the earth with fine little stitches of green. How you embroider the fields with flowers, and petit-point the beaches with sand and shells. I think of the brilliant, ever-changing tapestry of the trees.

Thank you for all this loveliness, Lord. For its patient artistry. When I take up my needle and thread the bright yarn, I feel very close to you.

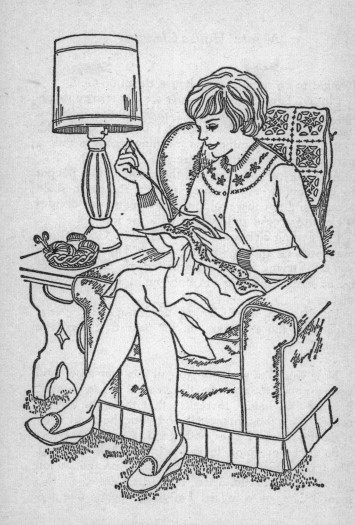

Mental House Cleaning

I've got to do some mental house cleaning, God.

I brood, I fret, I stew. I waste all this energy carrying on little dialogues with people who've offended me, or who aren't doing what I think they should. Just listen to my mind this morning, going a mile a minute along the paths of misery.

And not just the misery of the moment. No, it's got to go plowing up the past, finding things to scold about. And not just scolding other people—it decides it's got to accuse and quarrel with me too.

I'm getting sick and tired of all this, God. It gets me nowhere and it wears me out. The people I'm mentally trying to reform aren't being changed, not by an eyelash. While I'm only multiplying my own distress.

I don't even benefit by my tirades against myself! Especially those things of the past that can't be helped.

Now God, I'm going to stop all this nonsense. And you're going to give me the power. Prayer power. Because I've begun to realize that the only way to order, "Out, thoughts, out!" and *keep* them out is by replacing the bad ones with good. And by praying.

So first I'm going to call on you. Ask for help. Then ask a blessing—yes, a *blessing*—on the person I'd otherwise battle. Then, instead of doing all this mental damage to myself I'm going to improve myself: learn something, recite something, practice something. A poem, a psalm, a quotation, a formula, another page of French. And when I run out of things to learn or practice I can always pray.

Thanks for giving me a hand with this mental house cleaning, God. I expect to get a lot of learning done, and get in a lot of praying.

Let Me Say "Yes" to New Experiences

Lord, don't let me be afraid to say "Yes" to new experiences. New places to go, new people to meet, new things to learn. Don't let me be a coward about trying things—new friends or new foods, new books or new music, new inventions, new ideas.

Sure, it's safer and a lot less trouble just to chug along in the same old rut. But that way lies age and stagnation. The young are so willing to *try* things. And while you didn't design us to stay young forever, if I'd created a world so gloriously full of creatures, places and adventures, I'd be sad to see my children cowering in corners, refusing to discover its surprises—at least until they had to.

Lord, thank you for helping me overcome sheer laziness and dread:

Dread of travel. Half-eager to go, half-miserable before the complexities and problems any trip presents. How much easier not to have to shop, pack, cope with tickets and arrangements. Just to stay home where things are familiar. Yet how grateful I am for having made the effort. My life's store of friendships, knowledge and memories is enriched because of every trip I've taken.

Dread of sports, physical challenge. Learning to swim and dive and skate, learning to ski and ride and play tennis. The voices that whimper and warn, especially as we get older: "The water's cold," or "You might get hurt," or "Stay here where it's warm and cozy. Who *needs* this?" Lord, don't let me give up the things I already can do, or give in to the voices that would stop me from at least attempting new ones. The back porch may be more secure, but the fun is in jumping the fences . . .

Dread of meeting new people. Even the friends now so dear to me were once sometimes frightening strangers. Yet you led me to them, Lord, often against my own resistance. And my life would be empty without them.

God, don't ever take away my courage to try things.

Guard me from recklessness and folly, from foolishly sampling something just because it's "in" but that I know is wrong. Yet with that sole exception, keep alive my enthusiasm, my curiosity and daring. Let me say "Yes" to new experiences.

I'm Tired of Being Strong

Forgive me, Lord, but I'm tired of being some of the things I've tried so hard to be.

I'm tired of being so capable, so efficient. I'm tired of the compliment, "If you want to get something done ask a busy person." (Guess who?)

I'm tired of being considered so patient and understanding that people dump their troubles (and their kids) on me.

I'm tired of being so cheerful. I want to be free to be cross and complain and not get a "buck up, old girl," routine. I'm tired of being my husband's faithful partner and helpmate instead of his playmate.

I'm tired of being considered so independent, so strong.

Sometimes, at least sometimes, Lord, I want to be weak and helpless, able to lean on somebody, able to cry and be comforted.

Lord, I guess there are just times when I want to be a little girl again, running to climb on my mother's lap.

The Missing Ingredient

Lord, I have all the ingredients for happiness in my life. A lovely home, a wonderful husband. Children, friends, health. Why then is there such a sense of vacancy in me? Why this glum feeling of futility, even sometimes despair?

It's as if I keep expecting something glorious to happen that part of me is afraid is never *going* to happen. Some added flavor that's lacking, some challenge. Snug and safe and lucky (oh, so lucky) I press my disconsolate nose against the shining picture windows of my nest.

I want a parade to come by instead of just seeing kids climbing off a school bus. I want a limousine full of mysterious and exciting people to sweep up to the curb instead of a fuel-oil truck. I want the world to cry, "Come out, come out, you brilliant, beautiful thing! Why are you wasting yourself there?"

I want some glamor, some drama, some attention. I want to do something *important*.

I know, Lord—yes, yes, I know that making a home, raising a family *are* important. And that when the house is cold, better a fuel-oil man than a diplomat. So give me a sensible scale of values, give me patience.

But don't make me too sensible either. Don't give me too much patience. Maybe this is a "divine discontent" to keep me from getting sluggish, complacent. Maybe this hunger for some missing ingredient in my life is simply a way of telling me: "If you want something exciting to happen, you've got to *make* it happen." . . . Join a theater group or start one. Take a class or teach one. Find a job or create one. Sing, paint, write, dance. Help others who don't have the things I'm so blessed with and don't always appreciate.

Maybe you *meant* women like me to grow restless, in order to give our full measure to a world that has been so good to us.

How Have I Grown as a Person?

Lord, help me to remember that true growth is always an inward thing. Growth of the secret self—growth of the mind, growth of the spirit. And that no one can possibly take anyone's measure of progress but himself.

These old college friends we've just visited in their palatial home . . . Their walls are full of trophies from golf and tennis matches, souvenirs from travel . . . They belong to the best clubs. Every son and daughter has a car and a couple of horses and goes to the finest schools. They're wonderful people, Lord, and they've climbed the ladder of success so fast it makes the head swim (especially when you're looking up from a lower rung).

It's hard not to feel discontent with our own progress. Hard not to be filled with envy.

Rid me, please rid me of these unworthy emotions. Strip me of this too handy, deceptive materialistic measure. Give me a gauge for true growth, God— growth of the mind and spirit. And remind me its only accuracy and value is when I use it on myself.

Looking back, am I a better person than I was a few years ago? Have I outgrown intolerance? How many plaques and cups could I claim for faults overcome? How far have I traveled in patience, how much have I gained in compassion? And what have I *learned*? About books and art and music and politics and people? About myself and the world around me? How much do I *know*?

I don't want to be self-righteous or unrealistic about this, Lord. Surely it's natural and right to want more for ourselves and our children. To set economic goals. But don't let me be so dazzled by the outward symbols of success that I lose sight of the inner achievements.

And one important achievement, right now, will be to rejoice in our friends' success. To love them and ask you to bless them.

Thank you for their progress, Lord. And for our own.

Program My Mind for Optimism

Help me to be more optimistic, God. To smile more, laugh more, make more joyful, affirmative statements. Not only for my own sake but for the sake of the children.

How can they feel good about the world and themselves and being alive, especially in this great country, if I'm always singing the blues?

How can I expect them to respect or love things if I continually tear them down? How can they grow into happy, healthy, confident, success-likely people?

Don't let me be a phony. Help me to be honest about good and bad as I see it. (The world is *not* all sweetness and light, as they discover only too soon.) But guard my tongue. Whether my subject be the state of the nation, their school, this house, the neighbors, our relatives, their dad, or them, or *me* . . . let me admire and rejoice more often than I criticize.

Help me to cancel out negative statements and even negative mental dwelling on sickness and troubles and the general lousiness of life. Put good strong glowing words and images in their place. For you made our minds like perfect computers (too perfect sometimes). Whatever this perfect instrument is fed, it spews right back.

And you have given parents this subtle but awesome power to shape our children's lives. However they grow and change, they can never escape the early daily programming of their minds.

Please help me to fill my mind and the minds of my children with the ideas and attitudes that will help them stride confidently and cheerfully into this marvelous adventure, life.

Moving the Rock of Gibraltar

Thank you, dear God, and hooray! That I've finally moved the Rock of Gibraltar.

My husband has promised to remodel the kitchen —at last. He's drawn up the plans and made the first phone calls. He's even knocked out that old pantry and is talking about appliances I didn't think we could afford.

Now that he's in action there will be no stopping him.

But I can't help wondering, God, why you made so many husbands so stubborn? Why it takes them so long to *start*?

I just know (and am grateful to know) that if a wife keeps chipping away long enough (hopefully without actually nagging or having a fit about it) the day eventually comes when the rock gives way. And when it does, the results often surpass anything we dared to dream.

But maybe obstinance is an important part of that rock's nature, Lord; maybe you meant him to be that way—that sturdy rock, the man who supports his family. The rock's got to be hard so the assaults of life won't break it—our fights, our problems, our demands, as well as those of his job. It's got to be strong enough to protect us. But we know that we can lean on it, depend on it, it will be there when we need it.

Meanwhile, thank you for the times when this dear obstacle finally yields. Hooray and Hallelujah! I've moved the particular Rock of Gibraltar you gave me, God.

Make Me a Better Listener

Please make me a better listener, Lord. Help me to correct my conversational faults.

Give me more patience with my children's long-winded tales. Don't let me cut them off, or interrupt to correct their grammar or stop to challenge seemingly foolish ideas. Guard me against the temptation to overpower them with my "authority"—my greater experience, my larger stock of words. When we argue, don't let me always win.

Kids are so eager for an audience, Lord, so anxious to try out their thoughts. Don't let me diminish their pleasure. Open my ears and my heart to their efforts. How can I understand or guide or even enjoy them if I'm not a good and gracious listener?

Help me to listen, really listen, to my husband, Lord.

Like other wives, I often complain that "he never tells me anything." Yet how often has he tried to tell me things I've been too preoccupied to hear? I'm ashamed to admit it, but it's as if a little button in my mind tunes him out. I start mentally redecorating the bedroom or planning a luncheon. Or, to make sure he thinks I'm interested, I rush in with questions that rush *him*.

Lord, make me more patient in listening to my husband—and more alert. Give me more genuine interest in the things he wants to share—no matter how unimportant they may seem. You know how I long to communicate with him on deeper levels. Yet how can this happen unless I form the habit of truly listening to him?

Lord, help me to listen carefully to other people.

In too many conversations I just mark time rehearsing what *I* am going to say when I can break in. It's a common fault, but that's no excuse. Please stop these inner voices yammering for attention. Help me to give my complete attention to what is being said. I can gain so much, learn so much and give so much just by listening to others.

So many people's greatest need is someone to talk to. Someone who'll listen as if he or she really cares. Make me that kind of listener, Lord. A person who can "listen with the eyes and hear with the heart," as the old saying goes.

Please make me a better listener.

I Can't Understand My Daughter Any More

I just can't understand my daughter any more, God. And she can't understand me.

We used to be so close, we used to be such friends. Even when we had our differences she'd come flying back to me.

But now, though there are still moments of sweetness and laughter, times when we can talk, those times are so few. I don't understand her silences, Lord, her locked door, the secrets she keeps from me. And when we do talk there is so much crossness and tension and criticism. Often outright hostility.

Where has my little girl gone, God? What have I done to drive her away?

And you, Lord, seem to tell me:

She's going where you went, where all girls go: To find herself. And you haven't driven her away. Life is beckoning to her, and she must follow. This is what you've really been preparing her for, isn't it? To be strong enough to find her way.

But it hurts, God. I love her so much. Why must she make it so hard for me?

And clear and true I hear the answer. The only possible answer: *Because it is so wonderful having a daughter. Otherwise, you couldn't bear to let her go!*

The Box in the Attic

This box of college keepsakes, God. I don't know whether to laugh or cry, going through them. I don't know whether to wrap them up tenderly again or pitch them out.

The cups and medals so tarnished, the photographs of glory, hopelessly dated, poor things. And these dry, faded flowers . . . how could I ever have thought their colors would last? They're ghost flowers now. This whole box is filled with nothing but ghost memories, ghost promises . . .

The speaking contests won. The plays when everybody said I had so much talent, ought to go to New York, become a star. Here are some of the old programs, here is the dusty velvet costume I wore as Desdemona. I hold it up forlornly, half amused, half guilty—I couldn't even get into it any more!

"Promises, promises," as the saying goes. Promises unfulfilled. And I wonder—have I failed life, Lord? Or has life failed me?

Or has there been any failure at all?

How do I know I'd ever have gotten to Broadway if I'd tried? Or become a star? Or been any happier if I had? And isn't the role I'm playing now just as important as any I'd have there? (The work is steadier, that's sure, and the rewards, though less spectacular, are surely a lot more lasting.)

So I wonder, trying to sort out this box in the attic, what should I be feeling—regret, or relief? Should I weep for my wasted talents, or should I be thankful that I've avoided the grim old-fashioned work and heartbreak it takes to succeed on the stage? (Not that there isn't plenty of that in being a wife and mother! And I *am* a star . . . well, anyway a co-star of this family.)

Yet something nags at me yet, Lord. A restlessness I can't rationalize away. These tarnished, tattered, faintly ludicrous souvenirs—they are a kind of mute accusing testimony. I did have talent once. And talent is precious, talent means responsibility. Like that story in the Bible, when you give somebody talent you don't expect it to be buried.

Have I buried my talent, Lord, or only put it away for safekeeping? Surely there are places where I can use my talent still. And for better purposes now than just to satisfy my own ambition. Surely, without neglecting anybody, I can find outlets right here— little theater, coaching children, helping out with plays for charity.

I can't repolish the loving cups, let out the costumes, refurbish these souvenirs. But I can polish up my own gifts, let out my own horizons, reactivate *me!* Instead of mooning over past triumphs, I can get going on tomorrow's.

Thank you, Lord, for leading me to this box of keepsakes in the attic.

Give Me the Love to Let Them Go

Lord, sometimes I love my children so much it seems I can't ever bear to let them go.

"Hurry back!" my heart cries after them almost every time they leave, whether for camp or a date or just the daily trudging off down the walk for school.

No matter what the confusion we've just been through—the frantic scramble for books or money or a missing sweater, no matter the chaos, the noise, even the quarrels, something inside me goes scurrying after them with last minute words of love and warning. And the urgent unspoken plea: "Come back soon."

And when they are all gone at once, God, like right now . . . Though you know how I revel in the peace and freedom, yet there is this aching emptiness inside me too.

And sometimes, alone with their father, I have this sense of some awful preview: Of loneliness and boredom. Of a life without purpose and meaning. Of two people haunting the mailbox for letters, or waiting for the phone to ring . . . Or worse, a couple clinging to an unmarried son or daughter, unwilling to let the last one leave.

Lord, thank you for making me aware of this dread presentiment. It's like a signal telling me I've got to start weaning myself from my children. Not loving them any less, but ceasing to feast so continually on all they do. I realize I've got to start nourishing myself in other ways. New interests apart from them—help me to find them, God, starting now. Spur me to call that class I've been thinking of joining, that volunteer service that needs me. Things that will help me to grow as a person. There are a hundred unlocked doors and opportunities in my life, things I want to explore, things that challenge.

Now is the time to anticipate them. Now is the time to start finding them. Don't let me make excuses for myself—how busy I am, how much the children still need me. And guard me from these guilty, doubtful feelings already beginning to stir.

Brace me with the knowledge that the kindest, most generous thing I can do for my family is to begin to prepare for the time when they won't be coming back. A time when they won't have to feel guilty or selfish about poor old Mom whose world has collapsed.

Thank you for this insight, God. Give me the love to let my children go.

A Prayer for Energy

Please give me energy, Lord. Just plain old-fashioned energy. It takes so much just to crawl out of bed in the morning and get through the day. Physical and emotional energy.

Yes, I know and am grateful that I don't have to scrub clothes on a board, or beat rugs, or perform a lot of hard labors that my mother and grandmothers did. Yet I am assaulted from all sides by a lot of things they didn't have to cope with:

The energy-draining demands of clubs and committees and drives, and a society that insists I try to save it from its follies. A family that takes great bites out of me every day. A husband whose very work requires that I too be alert, strong, wise. That I entertain for him, be a credit to him, even as I try to fulfill a wife's perennial role of comforting and encouraging him.

All this plus work of my own that I love, sure, but that refuses to countenance weakness. That demands productivity—*energy*.

I sometimes get so *tired*, God. Despite tonics and vitamins and hormones, so excruciatingly, witlessly tired. I sometimes think I can't get through another twenty-four hours.

And then I turn to you like this and feel a quieting down. A sense of peace and reassurance. "Yes, you can, of course you can," an inner voice tells me. And

I realize at such times that I've got to take a little more time to replenish my energy.

To just—flop . . . rest. Be silent. Meditate . . . dream . . . or simply stare at the sky . . . drawing in energy. Energy from the sun . . . From the stars, so still and bright at night, so radiant and life-recharging.

Energy from the wind blowing across my face. Energy from the rain. Energy from the universe itself. Energy from you, the source of my own being.

Energy is there for me, God, always there for the taking. Help me to remember this and reach out for it, accept it, use it. Thank you for giving all of us this eternal, dependable, limitless source of energy.

Liberation

What is the true meaning of liberation, Lord?
Women's liberation . . . Any woman's liberation.

Help me to find my own true liberation.

From these children, this kitchen, this house, this
seemingly dead-end job. I flee the prison of my house
to work, and find I have merely shifted prisons.
There too, in so many ways, the bars are firm. Against
advancement, against genuine achievement. The gates
are locked. I find myself torn, looking back, compar-
ing prisons.

I try to escape them both—in a social life—clubs,
friends, parties. But the sense of freedom is brief and
often false. I sense the frenzy back of the bright, too
fervent contacts, the shallow conversation. As if
everybody else is fleeing too, trying to pack too much
into the hours before the paddy wagon comes to take
us back where we belong—in prison.

It's something like that, Lord. Wherever we go
we're scared of being found out: *I'm not as successful as they think—if they only knew how insecure I
am, how anxious . . . Nor as attractive—if they could
see me without my make-up—! . . . I'm not as kind
and radiant as I seem, not as generous, not as good
. . . If they knew me as I really am, would they even
like me?*

We're all trying to hide our shackles.

* * *

Maybe that's it, Lord. Maybe that's the real prison. Not the work we do or the place where we do it, but these self-doubts, self-punishments, tormentings. The secrets locked in the tight little cell inside ourselves.

We have sentenced our own souls to solitary confinement and blamed the world. We're afraid to be free because we don't feel worthy!

Liberate us, Lord. Love us enough, despite our faults and follies, to let us love and respect ourselves. Make us realize the true wonder and power of being a woman, no matter what we do. For then no barriers can confine us, there are no walls we cannot scale.

Surely this is the true freedom—to be free in spirit.

Thank you for giving us this key to our own liberation, Lord.

I Must Depend on Myself

Thank you, Lord, that there are so many people I can depend on for so many things. My husband and children. My neighbors and friends. The people with whom I work. I know I can count on any one of them—most of the time, at least—to do things for me, often without being asked. Just as they know they can count on me to help them.

But there is another person I must learn to depend on even more, Lord: *Myself*. You gave each of us areas of life where we *can't* lean on anybody else.

Nobody else can do our exercises, stick to our diets, study our courses, take our exams. Nobody else can read or write our books, sing our solos, dream our dreams, execute our plans. Nobody else can get our lives organized, productive and moving in the direction of our goals.

In short, Lord, no other person can keep my promises—to others or to me. For that, all that, I've got to depend on myself.

Help me to remember this. God, give me belief in myself and the will power to act on that belief. Thank you for gradually guiding me into habits that fortify that faith, so that at the end of each day I can realize: "I didn't let me down. I did what I promised myself!"

And even when I undertake too much, set my sights too high, project goals a little beyond my reach, help me not to get discouraged. Rather, to realize that delay doesn't mean defeat. Despite a hundred detours, I will keep driving in the right direction.

I will not quit. I will keep my commitments.

Thank you for giving me a clear, honest awareness of this, God, and the courage to live by that truth. Make me always able to depend on myself.

The Fragrance of Fall

Thank you, God, for the heady fragrance of fall.

This spicy scent of leaves and drying grasses, this perfume of the harvest—apples and grapes and orange pumpkins bright on roadside stands. As if the world is busily blending its wonders into some essence that haunts the soul even as it signals the year's end.

This nip and tingle of fall on a frosty morning, Lord, biting deep into the senses. This mellow fall fragrance on a sunny afternoon—stirring yet more serene . . . But in the evening, ah in the evening, when a new moon is rising and the smell of dinner lingers and children beg to scuff the leaves, hunting acorns for school—then the fragrance of fall is a kind of insistent presence, blood-invading.

It breathes of lost people far away in distant places, ancestors camping on ancient hillsides. It speaks of forests when our own country was mysterious and new. It echoes the smoke of fires in little log huts, with Indians lurking.

It speaks of home. It speaks of happiness.

Now . . . *now!* it seems to be urging. Be grateful for this moment. For home and husband and children and friends and all that you have and are. Breathe it, taste it, feel it—it holds the very essence of life, to be savored.

Thank you, God, for this heady fragrance of fall.

For All Warm Things

For all warm things of this season I thank you, Lord.

For the warmth of my house as I come in cold from shopping. For the fragrant warmth of my kitchen as I turn on the oven and sift and measure and stir and bake. For the snug warmth of the bedrooms where (finally, after much commotion) my children sleep. For the warmth of this cup of steaming coffee in my hand as I settle down (exhausted, and at last) before the fire that dances so warm and festive on the grate.

And for warm clothes, Lord. These slippers, this robe—all the untidy closets bursting. That car coat tossed across a chair. And the car itself, a warm car to take us places (once we get it *started*). And those warm places: the homes of neighbors, friends, a warm church to worship in.

And the warm people there. The warm smiles and greetings. The generosity and kindness of people everywhere.

I am full of this warmth, Lord. It comforts me, it calms me. It makes me feel a glow almost as rosy as the embers in the fireplace. I want all people to be warm and rested and at peace.

Thank you for this blessed season of warmth in the midst of so much that is chill and stormy. Let it draw all of us together against the coming cold.

Modern Pilgrims: Mothers

Thank you, God, for Thanksgiving.

Thank you for those incredible people, the Pilgrims, who taught us what it is to be grateful. Who, after all their hardships, still paused to count their blessings and to praise you for letting them survive another year.

I think of them as I drive to the airport to meet a son coming home from college (deploring the price of gas and mentally practicing arguments to keep that son and his dad from spending all day before the TV set).

Imagine being that grateful just for survival!

It makes me feel unworthy, Lord. Here am I with plenty of clothes, plenty to eat, a comfortable house with many appliances—and I'm not nearly as thankful as those Pilgrims were. Although we've had to do without a lot of things, we've never been really cold or hungry. Never homeless or threatened as many people still are, even today. (And not only in other parts of the world, but right here in the land our ancestors settled, as well.)

My heart aches for those people, Lord. As I count my own blessings I resolve to do more to translate that ache into action.

Yet, like the Pilgrims, I too should be thankful just to have survived another year. For the life of almost any mother *is* a matter of constant survival. Of battling enemies without and within. Of self-doubts and foolish broodings. Of anxieties and worries. Of budgets and bills and clutter; of getting up at night with children; of dashes to the hospital or the school. It's a series of conflicts and crises that sometimes seem beyond endurance.

Yet if, like those Pilgrims, we pause to look back, we are filled with surprised rejoicing.

How many hours of pride and pleasure and contentment we had, too. How many rewards and comforts. Your generosity overwhelms us. In retrospect we see the struggle as glorious, the triumph sweet.

"We made it, we made it!" we want to proclaim. "And look how richly blessed we are."

We discover, like our forefathers (and mothers) that a time of rest and Thanksgiving refreshes us, God. It refurbishes our strength for the adventure ahead, and renews our faith in ourselves and in you.

You have not failed us. We have not failed our families. Together we will not only survive but exult in another year.

A Mother's Wish-Gifts for Christmas

The family has all scattered on errands, Lord, and at last I can wrap their presents. But now, as I sit in this bright clutter of paper and ribbons, I keep thinking of other things, better things, I wish I could give them.

First, I'd love to put peace, world peace in a package. (What a marvelous present for all families everywhere that would be.) But since I can't, maybe I can try even harder to keep peace within this house. To manage less-hectic meals and bedtimes, to prevent or calm down its arguments and conflicts.

Help me in this, Lord.

And this fishing rod I'm struggling to make look nice for my husband, without revealing its secret. What would I like its clumsy package to include?

Freedom to *go* fishing more often, for one thing. But mostly freedom from worry. Worry about mortgages and car payments; about our health, the children's future, our happiness.

But as I sit pondering this impossible gift, you make me realize I *can* give him something very important that will help achieve that very thing: My consideration. Doing everything within my power to spare him.

Our sons, Lord. What would I like to tuck into their boxes along with the boots and shirts and football gear? For one of them, self-confidence, belief in his own abilities, more ease with girls. For the other, better grades so he'll get into the college he wants to attend.

How can I compensate for these gifts that I can't bestow? By more encouragement, more praise, by showing them every day how much I believe in them.

And my daughters, Lord. As I wrap the sweaters and tennis rackets, the books and records, the doll clothes I stayed up so late to finish for the littlest one . . . I can think of so much more I'd hand them if I could.

I'd like to give them poise and graciousness. Kindness and compassion. Courage for all occasions—for tests and dates and interviews, but especially the courage to be themselves whether it makes them popular or not.

Above all, I'd like to say, "Open your eyes and your arms to this priceless present: the wonder of being a woman today when so many careers are calling and you can still be a wife and mother if you want."

The list of my longings for my family is endless, Lord. I can't wrap up the things I really want. But one thing I can give all of them—though no box would ever be big enough to hold it. Something that's mine alone to give, as often as I want:

My love.

The Priceless Gift

Give me true generosity at Christmas, Lord. A generosity that doesn't get confused with pride or extravagance.

May this family's cards, our tree, our parties, our decorations, be all in the spirit of loving celebration of a glorious event, rather than the desire to impress.

Let me give with the zeal of my own children who will labor half the night to make something for somebody they love. Or who will spend every long-saved or hard-earned penny, not to show off, but because it is a glorious thing to give ungrudgingly, even at personal sacrifice.

Help me, above all, to remember that the family we honor and worship at Christmas were poor. Very poor. They couldn't have afforded a fine hotel had there been room. They were happy to take shelter in a hillside cave. They did not demand the best crib, the finest toys and garments for the child you sent. They were grateful to wrap him in swaddling clothes and place him in a manger.

God, fill me too with that same shining sense of gratefulness. So that it is not the price-tag-ridden emotions that dominate at Christmas, but joy in your priceless gift.

Grant me true generosity at Christmas, Lord. A generosity of spirit that is rooted in thankfulness.

The Christmas Spirit

Oh, Lord, it can't last, I know it can't last—this sense of joy I feel, this mounting sense of love and understanding and delight in all the world.

It is rising in me like a fountain. I want to dance with it, I want to sing. I want to draw all living creatures into its magical circle to share its radiance, to experience its wonder.

This gift of yours, this sweet inexplicable gift of the Christmas spirit. Why is it so long in coming to some of us? And why can't everyone have it always? Why must it be so brief?

Why must it dwindle and vanish when the season of Christmas is past and we have returned to the tasks and troubles of everyday? Why must peace and good will be limited to these beautiful days of celebration?

The Christmas spirit is like a baptism, Lord. It is your Holy Spirit, surely, baptizing us with the innocent joy of the newborn king. It makes us kings too for a little while. It makes us feel like newborn gods.

Oh, Lord, thank you for the Christmas spirit. And "Take not thy Holy Spirit from us," in the days when Christmas is past.

New Year's Eve

It's almost over, Lord. The old year's almost over.

In a few minutes the whistles and bells will proclaim it. "Forget it, it's over. Off with the old, on with the new!"

But I'm already a little homesick for the old year, Lord. I don't want it to be over, not really. I want to hang onto it a little longer. The happiness it held— the joys and surprises. Big important ones, yes, but the little ones too. Delights that were often too small or perhaps too frequent even to realize, to appreciate and savor before they vanished.

Even the pain and problems—somehow I want to cling to them too. I long to rush back, reclaim them. Handle them differently, be more careful, more patient, more generous, more wise. I don't *want* the New Year, Lord. I just want another chance at the old one!

But mostly I don't want to part with it just yet. For we loved it, whatever mistakes we made. It was ours, our life together.

But now the bells are clanging, the whistles are shrieking. People are laughing and singing—and I am caught up in the excitement too. "Don't look back," everything seems to be shouting. "Look ahead!"

And a great exhilaration courses through me as I realize: Yes, yes, they are right. How wonderful, that every year you present us with this great, new, shining package of time.

How promising its contents. How mysterious. How thrilling, challenging, in some ways almost frightening. Yet mainly how marvelous—that we can discover those contents only as we live them. Until we have stripped off the final wrapping of the final day and another year lies at our feet.

Revealed, completed, endured, enjoyed. But whole at last, and so—wholly and utterly ours.

Thank you that as we put the old year away with all the tattered and treasured Years Past, you always give us a new one to open.

Life is so dear. Each year is so dear. Each *day* is so dear. Thank you for every moment, Lord.

An American Woman's Prayer

Thank you, God. First and foremost that I'm a woman. What's more, an American woman—that luckiest of all possible beings. For nowhere else in the whole wide world could I be so respected, so cherished, so privileged (some people call it downright spoiled) and yet so free.

Thank you that I can vote or run for office (and win too). That I can marry or not, have children or not, work or not, and it's nobody's business but my own; there's nobody really to stop me but me.

Thank you that, although discrimination dies hard (men have run your world so long, God, and forgive me but you made men proud and slow to change), no doors are really closed to me. I can be a doctor—surgeon, dentist, vet. I can be a lawyer, I can be a judge. I can dance, swim, act—be an artist, drive a trick, umpire a baseball game. I can work in forests or harvest fields as well as offices if it suits me.

But, dear Lord, how I thank you that my government doesn't *make* me do any of these things. I can stay home and be a wife and mother if I please. I can be my own boss as I cook and sew and chase the kids and clean. (And while I'm at it, thank you for the marvelous conveniences that make keeping house in America easier than anyplace else on earth.)

* * *

Thank you, God, for the prosperity and plenty of this incredible country. The abundance of our resources—coal and oil and water and grain, and human energy and skill. For you know how hard we've worked to get where we are. Unlike the skeptical hireling of the parable, we didn't just bury the gifts you gave us, but plowed and sowed and sweat and made them bear fruit. And then, with arms and hearts overflowing, we rushed to the whole world's aid.

Thank you that we inherited not only our forefathers' and mothers' achievements but their generosity, their willingness to share. That never in all our history have we turned our back on another nation in need.

Thank you, God, that my children were born in this remarkable land. *Born free.* Daughters as well as sons, just as free as I am to do with their lives what they will.

Oh, help us truly to value that freedom, God, and guard it well. Don't let us take it for granted. Don't let us become weak, soft, vulnerable. So afraid of being considered old-fashioned, so eager to be sophisticated, modern, that we play into the hands of those who would take it away.

Don't let us discount it, downgrade it. And dear God, make us just as quick to praise our country's virtues and triumphs and blessings as we are to criticize. For who can do his best—man, woman, child or nation—if no credit is ever forthcoming? No appreciation—only blame?

Help us to stop criticizing *ourselves* so much, God.

Restrain our own breast beating. Help us to remember that no nation since the beginning of time has ever had even half the freedom and advantages we enjoy.

Light in us fervent new fires of patriotism, Lord.

Patriotism. A word of passionate honor in almost every country except the one that deserves it so much! Make us proud to be American patriots once again. Willing to shout our heritage from the housetops. Let us thrill once more to the sight of our star-spangled banner. May it fly from every flagpole, be honored in every schoolroom. Let us and our children pledge our allegiance to it wherever Americans gather, and sing the words of its anthem with love and thanksgiving.

Oh, Lord, dear Lord, remind us: We are so *lucky* to be Americans. And I'm so lucky to be an American woman.

To the Reader

I am frequently asked how I write these prayers.

Most of those you see have evolved from something I have personally prayed about, for myself or others. Years ago I fell into the habit of sharing everything that concerns me with God. I wanted to keep in touch with the one who created me and is letting me take this marvelous trip—life! Just to thank and praise him for it makes me more aware of its wonders; and to pour out problems, frustrations, and longings to him gives me release, reassurance, and guidance. And being a writer, I began to listen to the rhythms of my thoughts.

That is really the beginning of writing anything— the cadences of words, the mental patterns, sometimes unconscious, sometimes controlled. What ultimately appears on paper, whether a short story, poem, or prayer, starts first as an insistent little song in the head. Prayer for me became a kind of poetry I could not resist putting down. Particularly when I recognized that these things I was expressing were not unique.

Practically everything I talk to God about is universal. The common experience of almost every man and woman—especially woman. And it came to me that the things I was learning, both from prayer and from life itself, could be of help to other people. It was then I began to consciously structure my prayers in a form that others could identify with, as well. People who might not realize just how close God is to each of us, and how much help is available if we only seek it.

We do get help as we pray. Not only courage, comfort, and strength, but new understanding. There is a great deal of self-analysis in prayer, especially if we're honest and confess our faults. I think God uses this process to make us realize truths about ourselves and others; He gives us new insights for resolving our problems. I try to incorporate some of these insights and answers into many of the prayers, at least to plant the seed of solution.

Have I actually been through everything I write about? Well, I've pretty much run the gamut of human experience. And what I have been spared, I have lived vicariously, but intensely, through people close to me. I have not been divorced, but have suffered through divorces with my children. I have not lost a son or a husband, but my heart has been torn by these losses through family and friends. A true writer must empathize; a writer lives hundreds of lives in his own mind and flesh. A writer *knows how such things feel*. And one of his greatest responsibilities and privileges is to express those feelings on behalf of others.

For me, the greatest reward of all this are the letters that pour in saying: "You're talking about *me*. How did you know?" And "You've helped me." Every now and then such letters will be accompanied by an original prayer inspired by one of mine. Someone who's discovered the joy of this approach to God. I am always happy when this happens. Try it. It could add a new dimension to your own relationship with the author of us all.

Marjorie Holmes

ABOUT THE AUTHOR

MARJORIE HOLMES is the author of hundreds of short stories and articles which have appeared in *McCall's*, *Ladies Home Journal*, *Reader's Digest* and other prominent national magazines. Her column "Love and Laughter" was a popular feature of the Washington *Star* for twenty years, and another column, "A Woman's Conversations with God," has had a tremendous following in *Woman's Day*. Recently she resigned from writing both columns in order to write the screenplay for her novel *Two from Galilee* (a love story of Mary and Joseph), which is to be filmed on location in Israel. Her twenty books include *I've Got to Talk to Somebody, God; Who Am I, God?* and *How Can I Find You, God?* racking up such incredible sales that *The New York Times* called her "a literary phenomenon." Marjorie Holmes has taught writing courses at The Catholic University, Maryland University, Georgetown University and at numerous writers' conferences. The National Federation of Press Women named her their Woman of Achievement for 1972. She lives with her husband, Lynn Mighell, on a beautiful lake at Manassas, Virginia, where her hobbies include swimming, canoeing and water skiing. She is the mother of four children and has four grandchildren.

Heartwarming Books of Faith and Inspiration

☐ 24989-4	IN THE SHADOW OF A SONG, Willadeene	$3.50
☐ 24007-2	JUST LIKE ICE CREAM, Johnson	$2.50
☐ 24452-3	LIFE AFTER LIFE, Moody	$3.95
☐ 23928-7	THE SECRET KINGDOM, Robertson & Slosser	$3.50
☐ 25669-6	THE HIDING PLACE, Boom	$3.95
☐ 25345-X	THE RICHEST MAN IN BABYLON, Clason	$3.50
☐ 22886-2	JONI, Eareckson w/Musser	$2.95
☐ 22706-8	FASCINATING WOMANHOOD, Andelin	$3.95
☐ 23977-5	MEETING GOD AT EVERY TURN, Marshall	$3.50
☐ 23334-3	ACT OF MARRIAGE, LeHayes	$3.95
☐ 24786-7	CONFESSIONS OF A HAPPY CHRISTIAN, Ziglar	$2.95
☐ 25155-4	A SEVERE MERCY, Vanauken	$3.95
☐ 23363-7	MAN OF STEEL AND VELVET, Andelin	$3.95
☐ 25438-3	BIBLE AS HISTORY, Keller	$4.95
☐ 24471-X	THE HIGH COST OF GROWING, Landorf	$2.95
☐ 24563-5	HOW TO WIN OVER DEPRESSION, LeHaye	$3.95
☐ 23166-9	"WITH GOD ALL THINGS ARE POSSIBLE," Life Study Fellowship	$3.50
☐ 25009-4	GUIDEPOSTS TREASURY OF LOVE	$3.50
☐ 24028-5	HEALING, MacNutt	$3.95
☐ 25011-6	MYTHS TO LIVE BY, Campbell	$4.50

Buy them at your local bookstore or use this handy coupon for ordering:

Bantam Books, Inc., Dept. HF4, 414 East Golf Road, Des Plaines, Ill. 60016

Please send me the books I have checked above. I am enclosing $_____ (Please add $1.50 to cover postage and handling.) Send check or money order—no cash or C.O.D.'s please.

Mr/Ms _____

Address _____

City/State _____ Zip _____

HF4—1A/86

Please allow four to six weeks for delivery. This offer expires 7/86. Price and availability subject to change without notice.

BANTAM
SHOP·AT·HOME
C·A·T·A·L·O·G

Special Offer
Buy a Bantam Book
for only 50¢.

Now you can have an up-to-date listing of Bantam's hundreds of titles plus take advantage of our unique and exciting bonus book offer. A special offer which gives you the opportunity to purchase a Bantam book for only 50¢. Here's how!

By ordering any five books at the regular price per order, you can also choose any other single book listed (up to a $4.95 value) for just 50¢. Some restrictions do apply, but for further details why not send for Bantam's listing of titles today!

Just send us your name and address and we will send you a catalog!